WELCOME TO UNDERSHAW

A Brief History of Sir Arthur Conan Doyle : The Man Who Created Sherlock Holmes

By Luke Benjamen Kuhns

Paperback ISBN 978-1-78705-021-1
ePub ISBN 978-1-78705-022-8
PDF ISBN 978-1-78705-023-5

Published in the UK by MX Publishing
335 Princess Park Manor, Royal Drive, London, N11 3GX
www.mxpublishing.co.uk

Cover design by Brian Belanger.

This book is dedicated to each and every person who believed in and supported the restoration of Undershaw.

Acknowledgements

Steve Emecz, mate it is because of you I found my way to Undershaw on a rainy autumn day which ignited my passion for the restoration efforts of this beautiful estate. Thank you for all your hard work and efforts to see this cause through.

Janice, you are the best and wisest woman I have ever known. Thank you for always motivating and inspiring me to reach higher and not to not settle for second best. To me you will aways be *The* Woman.

Bonnie MacBird, you have been instrumental in seeing me through several projects. You are an incredible friend and colleague to have, and I value the guidance you have given me over the years. Thank you a million times over!

Sora Reyes (of The Baker Street Babes), it has been a privilege to work on this book with you! Thank you for all your incredible efforts.

I want to thank everyone at DFN Charitable Foundation and *Stepping Stones* - the work you do is amazing and empowering. Thank you for believing in this project, I am humbled to have had a small part in your plan for the revitalisation of Undershaw.

I would also like to thank

The Conan Doyle Collection, The British Library, The Wellcome Collection, The Francis Firth Collection, Peter Harrington Rare Books, and Roger Johnson for the kind use of the amazing photographs in your collections.

Introduction

This book on Undershaw signals not the end of a great story but the beginning of a new chapter in the life of this wonderful old house.

When I first saw Undershaw it stood neglected and derelict, with windows broken and rotting away, surrounded by overgrown vegetation that had swallowed up whole areas, so that no one could appreciate the wonderful views of the Surrey Hills that have now been revealed.

It was hard to imagine that Sir Arthur Conan Doyle had built this house for his family, which provided the base for his most productive literary period; he resurrected his character Sherlock Holmes, the most famous fictional detective in the world, and wrote his classic book "The Hound of the Baskervilles" along with many others. Conan Doyle and his wife Touie welcomed many famous literary, artistic and political friends and acquaintances to their home including Bram Stoker, J.M. Barrie, Virginia Woolf and H. Rider Haggard among many others. I hope new visitors will receive an equally warm welcome when they enter Undershaw today.

I was determined to do everything I possibly could to bring this home back to life and give it a real purpose. Now fully restored, Undershaw will provide a 'school that feels like home' for the many students with additional needs who will be helped at the school we have established on the site. It is also intended that it will be well used by the wider community including the many Conan Doyle and Sherlock Holmes enthusiasts who are welcome to visit in the years to come.

Richard Doyle, great nephew of Sir Arthur, wrote:

"I don't believe that Undershaw should be preserved in aspic, but lived in and laughed in…. If it is possible for some of this magical, special building to become the heart of a new school that contributes to the thriving community of Hindhead then I would be very happy".

The restoration and development of Undershaw has been a fascinating journey as we first peeled back the layers of the original house and then carefully pieced it back together for others to enjoy.

My Foundation will continue to act as custodian of Undershaw, ensuring it is well cared for and preserved for future generations. I am certain that you will thoroughly enjoy reading about Sir Arthur Conan Doyle and his life at Undershaw.

So turn the page and begin to explore the life of a literary genius!

David Forbes-Nixon
Chairman
DFN Charitable Foundation
August 2016

"I have had a life which, for variety and romance, could, I think,
hardly be exceeded." - A.C.D 1924

Introduction by Bram Stoker

In 1907, Bram Stoker travelled to Hindhead to interview Sir Arthur Conan Doyle. I find no better words for introduction than this segment of the interview between the two literary giants:

"My first book! That was written when I was six years of age! But if I am to tell you about myself, I suppose I had better begin at the beginning" The Speaker was lying on a chintz covered sofa in the pretty drawing-room of his house at Hindhead, down in Surrey.

The forenoon sun was streaming in through one of the mullioned windows, of which the bars were softened by the delicate fringe of green of the creepers which spread along them. The whole room was full of soft light, which showed the fine old furniture and the multitude of dainty knick-knacks to perfection. Even the many quaint and pretty pictures seemed to stand out from the walls. From where I sat the whole of the lovely valley, at the very head of which the house stand, lay before me. Due south it falls away, spreading wider as it goes, till the lines are lost in the distance, an endless sea of greenery. Far away there are ranges of hills piling up, one behind the other, in undulation of varying blue. Even the whole sweep of the horizon visible from our altitude is like a wavy sea. Nearer at hand the wonderful green of the valley is articulated by the minor curves and slopes, the trend of surrounding hills. The mighty carpet of green is of the fresh young bracken, whose shoots seem close, are like little croziers wrote in emerald. Against this the rising pine trees seem like dark masses. Close to us, beyond the vivid patch of tennis lawn, are some masses of colour which are simply gorgeous amid the expanse of green. Great shrubs of yellow broom, clumps of purple rhododendron, luxuriant alder, with masses of snowy flowers starred in their own peculiar green. An expanse which, whether seen from near or far, in unity or detail simply ravishes the eye with its myriad beauties....that wide expanse seen beyond this foreground of idyllic beauty. Undershaw Home at Hindhead."

It is this very special place which we will visit in this book, a house whose halls and rooms I, too, have passed through. In the process we'll learn something about its designer and famous resident, Sir Arthur Conan Doyle — his life, his times, and what Undershaw meant to him.

---

¹Article from *The Daily Chronicle*, Published Feb 14th,1904. *http://www.bramstoker.org/nonfic/doyle.html*

Chapter 1

The Early Life of Arthur Conan Doyle

Who is Arthur Conan Doyle, what is Undershaw, and how do they relate? For many, Arthur Conan Doyle is the man who wrote the Sherlock Holmes stories — the detective in the funny deerstalker who always smoked a pipe and had a bumbling sidekick, Doctor Watson.

Yes, Doyle is the creator of Sherlock Holmes, but Sherlock Holmes wearing a deerstalker is never mentioned in any of the stories (only seen in illustrations) nor did Doctor Watson bumble. We have the 1940's Basil Rathbone films to thank that for that misconception.

Arthur Conan Doyle did far more than just write detective stories. He had a passion for writing historical works of knights and chivalry, chilling horror tales, plays, and even took up his pen to write about issues of politics and war. He lived a full life as an avid sportsman, adventurer, journalist and family man. But there is no denying that his (personally least favourite) creation, Sherlock Holmes, is, by far, his most enduring legacy.

Now you may be asking 'What is Undershaw?' If you're holding this book in your hand you probably already know. But let's pretend you don't.

Undershaw was the home of Arthur Conan Doyle between 1897-1907. The house in Hindhead is nestled in the side of a hill surrounded by tall green trees just off the main road. When you walk down the drive towards the house there is a sense of awe, almost as if you have found your way into a lost haven. You can look South and see the rolling Surrey hills stretching for miles until they fade into white. You can find adventure hiding in the woods, or you can lay a blanket on the ground and gaze at the bright blue sky and cotton ball clouds as they roll above. Undershaw is serene. As you wander the grounds you understand why Conan Doyle purchased the land and built a house here. Though it was not only the scenic view which inspired his ten year habitation.

But, in order to tell Undershaw's story I need to tell Conan Doyle's story. So, let's go back to a suitable beginning. Back to 1820

The Beginning of the Story

John Doyle, Sir Arthur's grandfather, was a political caricaturist. He married Marianna Conan in February 1820. The two had seven children together: Annette, James, Richard, Henry, Francis, Adelaide, and Charles. On December 11, 1839, tragedy befell the Doyle family when Marianna died of a heart disease. John Doyle was left with seven children aged between 7 to 18. Annette, at only 18 stepped in to help run the house with the help of her Aunt Elizabeth.

John Doyle made sure the children were taught the skills of pencil and brush. There was *"art in the blood"* that pulsed through the Doyle family. John's youngest son, Charles Doyle, father of Sir Arthur, also became an artist — a painter as well as a cartoonist.

Charles moved to Edinburgh, Scotland where he married Mary Foley, a seventeen-year-old Irish lass. She was small (five foot one inch), but a sturdy and charming woman. She was also a French scholar with a deep interest in heraldry.

On May 22, 1859, at II Picardy Place, Mary gave birth to a son, Arthur Ignatius Conan Doyle. At the time of Arthur's birth, Britain had led the charge of the Industrial Revolution sweeping Europe. It was a thrilling time to be alive; with promise and adventure around every corner as the Empire encircled the globe.

The child grew to be the light of his mother's life, her 'idol'. It was no secret that Arthur, a boy prone to smiling and rare to cry, was Mary's favourite. "Well, I suspect Mary blows his trumpet enough," John Doyle once remarked to his brother Richard "Dicky" Doyle.[2] And for all the adoration Mary poured over Arthur, he, too, returned that affection.

Mary Doyle was a proud woman and proud of her heritage. She instilled in young Arthur the importance of their lineage. Arthur's childhood was deeply impacted by thoughts of

Conan Doyle's mother at the age of 30.

chivalry and heraldry. Young Arthur took pride, just like his mother did, in these thoughts, and later remarked humorously of his boyish hubris: "I would sit swinging my knickerbocker legs, swelling with pride….as I contemplated the gulf which separated me from all the other little boys who swang their legs upon tables."

As were many who later turned to writing, Arthur was encouraged by his mother to read from a very early age. Sir Walter Scott's *Ivanhoe* was the starting point for his desire to read. Arthur would go through book after book and was particularly attracted to adventure stories. It was no surprise that he would soon attempt to write something of his own. Arthur once recalled his early years saying, "During these first ten years I was a rapid reader, so rapid that some small library with which we dealt gave my mother notice that books would not be changed more than twice a day."[4] Arthur was avid about his stories and devoured the books given to him. He also said, "My tastes were boylike enough, for Mayne Reid was my favourite author, and his *Scalp Hunter* my favourite book."

At the age of six, he wrote his first story about a 'Tiger and a Man', but which one was the hero of the story is long forgotten. He told his mother once, "It was easy to get people into scrapes, but not so easy to get them out again, which is surely the experience of every writer of adventures."

At seven he attended Newington Academy in Edinburgh, but at eight he was enrolled at Hodder House, the preparatory school for Stonyhurst, at the urge of his Uncle who wished him to have a Jesuit education.

This was not for religious purposes but rather to help the boy get into a good public school in England. Stonyhurst was a strict school, and where Arthur felt he did not get enough care. He recalled the extreme discipline that was inflicted upon the students who misbehaved. Boys would be slapped on the hand a minimum of nine times by an Indian-rubber said to be the size of a boot's sole. Arthur was not free of trouble making, but the trouble he made came as a result of defense. "If I was more beaten than others it was not that I was in any way vicious, but it was that I had a nature

[2] *The Life of Sir Arthur Conan Doyle, John Dickson Carr, p6, Carroll & Graf Publishers, New York, 2003.*

[3] *The Adventures of Arthur Conan Doyle, Russell Miller, p24, Harvill Secker, London, 2008.*

[4] *Memories and Adventures and Western Wanderings, pg6, Cambridge Scholars Publishing, Newcastle upon Tyne, 2009.*

which responded eagerly to affectionate kindness (which I never received), but which rebelled against threats and took a prevented pride in showing that it would not be cowed by violence."

It was at Stoneyhurst that Arthur found he had a knack for writing, which not only surprised him but his teachers who, truth be told, had little faith in Arthur's future. But Arthur, being a boy raised on heroic tales of chivalry, did not allow the teachers' opinions to thwart his endeavours. When it came time for Arthur to graduate Stonyhurst it was agreed that he would spend a year in Feldkirch attending Stella Matutina - a Jesuit college - in order to work on his German and expand his academic possibilities before he would attend London University.

When Arthur had completed his studies and returned to his family, he found things vastly changed, much to his consternation. His father had retired, and had turned to drink. His sister Annette was off in Portugal working as a governess, and a man by the name of Dr Bryan Charles Waller had taken up residence in the family home. Arthur felt this man, Waller, had usurped a leading role in the family. As Arthur was away and his father lost to drink, Waller, who was an Oxford-educated man and published poet, had stepped in and seemed to have won the affection of Mary Doyle.

In spite of the animosity between them, one good thing came to Arthur from this interloper. Waller was the one who suggested to Arthur that he pursue a medical career. Mary was pleased when Arthur returned to Edinburgh and announced he would not go to London University but to

Edinburgh University to study medicine.

While Arthur was not a fan of Waller, he did take advice from him before taking the entrance exams. Despite this, Waller does not get a single mention by name in Arthur Conan Doyle's autobiography: *Memories and Adventures*. But in any case, Waller's advice proved useful. In October 1876 Arthur began his medical education at University of Edinburgh Medical School. It was not to be an easy journey.

Chapter 2

University, Doctor Bell & the SS *Hope*

When Arthur returned from Germany he needed to obtain a scholarship for his studies. He spent one month in preparation and to his relief was awarded the Grierson bursary. The sum would be £40 for two years and would cover many of his costs. However, when he attempted to claim his scholarship he was informed that there was a clerical error and that scholarship only went to art students. Arthur hoped he could win the next scholarship, but it too was already claimed. Eventually he was given a pittance of £7. "It was a bitter disappointment," Arthur recalled, "I had a legal case, but what can a penniless student do, and what sort of college career would he have if he began by suing his University for money?"

Arthur's time at the University of Edinburgh not only built his foundation as a doctor but also provided him with some of his key inspirations for several of his most beloved fictional characters. It was during his time here that he met Doctor Joseph Bell, the man who inspired the character of Sherlock Holmes. It was also here that he met Professor William Rutherford, said to be an eccentric man with a booming voice and thick black beard, and zoologist Sir Charles Wyville Thomson who traveled aboard the H.M.S. Challenger. These men would be the foundational inspiration for the character of Professor Challenger.

Arthur was an active young man. Sports and games were always of keen interest to him. He played forward for the Rugby team at his University, had a fondness for Cricket, and dabbled in boxing and football. "I had an eager nature which missed nothing in the way of fun which could be gathered, and I had a great capacity for enjoyment. I read. Played games all I could. I danced, and I sampled the drama whenever I had a sixpence to carry me to the gallery."[5]

The University of Edinburgh's Faculty of Medicine had grown exponentially during the five years prior to Arthur's enrolment. The student body grew in numbers, too, swelling to more than a thousand. There were certain disadvantages to this. Professors found themselves overworked and taking on student-assistants to help carry the teaching load. This proved risky, as it meant the students sometimes received an uneven education. In fact, Arthur calculated that only 400 out of 1000 students actually graduated.

---

[5] *The Adventures of Arthur Conan Doyle, Miller, pg 48*

While academically challenging, Edinburgh did not offer the quality of student life that Oxford or Cambridge could. For one thing, the University had no social facilities, nor halls of residence. Students needed to live at home or find accommodation elsewhere. The students not only arranged what classes they wished to attend and exams to sit, but they also paid their fees directly to those lecturing, the latter probably being rather enticing to modern-day lecturers.

To succeed in this environment, students needed to be persistent, hungry for knowledge, and self-disciplined. There was no sliding by. But young Arthur was up to the task. Pressed to support himself and help his family, he had a very ambitious goal. As soon as he had completed two years of medical studies, he planned to cram a full year of classes into half a year so that he could quickly go out as a medical assistant and start earning a wage. Arthur's determination was demonstrated early, and served him well throughout his life.

Doctor Joseph Bell

DR JOSEPH BELL
Latest Photograph by Horsburgh

One of Arthur's most influential lecturers was Doctor Joseph Bell. In his early 40's at the time of Arthur's studies, Bell was already a legend among the students. He was a tall, hawk-nosed man with grey eyes, a description later given to Sherlock Holmes. And the similarity did not end there. His mastery of observation and deduction appeared to give him clairvoyant powers. One almost might say *superpowers*. He had the amazing ability to study a patient almost casually but then deduce remarkably accurate facts and diagnoses almost instantly. The accuracy of his assessments, all achieved by a minute study of details and backed by a prodigious amount of stored facts, stunned both students and patients. The effect was heightened because he was, as Sherlock Holmes was later described, a true showman when teaching his students.

A famous Bell trick was this: he presented his class with a bottle filled with an unknown amber liquid. He would tell the student it was an extremely vile drug and pressed that they taste it because it would be crucial that they know the taste. Bell assured them that he would of course not wish to impose anything upon his students that he himself would not do. So holding up the bottle, he dipped his finger into it and gave the amber liquid a taste. He shuddered with disgust.

The students would smirk and laugh at him, only to gulp when they realised it was now their turn. The rest of the class proceeded to follow their teacher's example. You can see them approach the great teacher one by one. "Go on," Bell might say assuredly to the students with a smirk of his own on his face as they dipped their reluctant fingers in the liquid, and softly chuckle to himself as they grimaced and shuddered at the foul taste.

Once the class had all tried it, Dr. Bell expressed his disappointment in the students' ability to observe! He pointed out that he had dipped his <u>index</u> finger into the bottle but stuck his <u>middle</u> finger into his mouth, therefore not actually tasting the liquid. The class saw, but they did not observe. It is easy to see why he enjoyed playing this little joke on his students; eager minds are often very gullible in certain situations, though I doubt they found it as humorous as he.

Arthur later recounted another instance of Bell's remarkable powers. He was able to deduce that a patient "was a soldier, non-commissioned officer recently discharged from a Highland regiment station in Barbados." When asked how he could possibly know this, Bell replied, "The man was a respectful man but did not remove his hat. They do not in the army, but he would have learned civilian ways had he been long discharged. He has an air of authority and he is obviously Scottish. As to Barbados, his complaint is elephantiasis, which is West Indian and not British, and the Scottish regiments are at present in that particular island." When it is explained the magic is gone, and it appears so very simple. It is so with Holmes as well. In *A Study in Scarlet*, one easily sees the similarity to Bell's "performances" and Holmes's own deductions about Dr. Watson.

As well as being a renowned centre for medical studies, Edinburgh was fertile ground for many future writers. J. M. Barrie, who wrote *Peter Pan* was among Arthur's contemporaries. Robert Louis Stevenson, author of *Treasure Island* and *The Strange Case of Doctor Jekyll and Mr Hyde*, was missed by Arthur by just one year. Stevenson left June of 1875, but it is always possible that Arthur brushed passed him in the local tavern, Rutherfords on Drummond Street. Or so he liked to think.

Finances continued to be an issue for Arthur. While he allocated himself a small sum for lunch, enough for a mutton pie, he'd often relinquish his lunch money to a used book store, a vice shared by many a writer. According to plan, Arthur crammed his studies into fewer months and in 1878, advertised his services as a doctor's assistant. This began Arthur's struggling start in the field of medicine.

Young Arthur was fired from this first job within three weeks and received no fee for his work. Disappointed and unsure where to go, he decided to travel to London to see his family until he found his next post.

Soon enough he found work. He took up an assistant role aiding a Doctor Elliott in a village near Shrewsbury. It was here that Arthur's confidence got a strong boost. An incident at a nearby house resulted in a victim with a severe head wound. A cannon had misfired and shrapnel had been lodged in the man's skull. Doctor Elliott was away, leaving Arthur alone to respond. It was a gruesome sight with blood and torn flesh. The patient's skull was exposed and there was the possibility of causing brain damage. But Arthur kept his cool and managed to successfully remove the shrapnel, leaving the patient's brain intact, stop the bleeding, and seal the wound. This was certainly the assurance that he needed. He was no amateur.

Next Arthur took up a post in Birmingham working for Dr Reginald Ratcliffe. It was hard work and long hours but he was finally being paid a decent wage. While employed by Dr Ratcliffe, Arthur began writing short stories. In 1879 *Chambers Journal* accepted Arthur's story: *The Mystery of Sasassa Valley*. He then wrote *The Haunted Grange of Goresthorpe*, a comedy/horror narrative, and several other stories including *The American's Tale*.

Arthur was endowed with a desire for adventure. Around this time he had the stirring to become a naval surgeon and, as providence would have it, a position opened up when a friend named Claude Currie was unable to fulfill a post onboard the steam-whaler SS *Hope*.

Captained by John Gray, the SS *Hope* would take Arthur into the cold arctic for seven months on a sealing and whaling cruise paying a decent salary of £50. This adventure began in February of 1880.

Young Arthur stepped eagerly aboard, knowing that as the 'new man' he would need to prove himself, and to gain the crew's respect. The challenge was quick to arrive. On his first night aboard he got into an altercation with the steward, Jack Lamb. The crew wanted to see what this young doctor could do. Would he really survive with them in the wild arctic? A fistfight ensued. By the end of the brawl Arthur had blackened the tough steward's eye — a feat which won him the crew's respect for the remainder of his time on board.

Lamb went on to say about Arthur, "He's the best Surgeon we've ever had — he's blacked my eye". By the end of his adventures on the SS *Hope*, Arthur felt a new sense of confidence, declaring that he had finally changed from a 'big, straggling youth' into a 'powerful, well-grown man'.

When Arthur returned from his Arctic ventures on this high note, it was now time for his University finals. But alarmingly, he found the family situation had deteriorated further. They had moved yet again, and Mr Waller was now paying the yearly rent of £60 for the family. His father, Charles, was further decimated by alcohol, and after some discussion, it was agreed that Charles be sent to Blairerno, a mental health "resort". This was, everyone knew, a kind of asylum.

Saddened but undaunted. Arthur would move into a new phase of his life.

Chapter 3

Doctor Arthur Conan Doyle, Portsmouth, Early Writings & Touie

Freshly graduated with decent marks, and a veteran of an Arctic adventure, Doctor Arthur Conan Doyle was twenty-two, and looking for work. When there were no immediate posts in the Hospitals, his options included joining the Army, Navy, and the Indian Service. Being the man of adventure that he was, he also applied for a ship's surgeon post aboard a passenger liner.

He duly took employ with African Steam Navigation Company on board the *Mayumba* for the moderate sum of £12 a month. Arthur stepped aboard the vessel wide eyed, hoping it would recreate his grand adventures on the SS *Hope*. He pictured visiting strange new lands, thrilling ports, and meeting savages. These hopes were quickly dashed. This time there were no fists fights to prove his worth, no blackened eyes, or anything of the sort. It was a wholly unremarkable voyage.

The tedium was made worse by relentless heat. One day, in an attempt to relieve himself from the soaring temperatures, and against advice, he dove into the water for a little swim. The bright sun beat down on him as he waded through warm but refreshing waters. To Arthur he was doing nothing senseless, that was until he climbed back on board the ship. Looking out into the water he saw the triangular shape of a dorsal fin ripping through the water. He quickly realised it was a deadly shark! Arthur had little doubt that the shark was on the hunt, and it made his blood run cold. "Several times in my life I have done utterly reckless things with so little motive that I found it difficult to explain them to myself afterwards. This was one of them," Arthur once remarked.

On January 14, 1882, the *Mayumba* returned from its long journey from England to Africa and back. By this time Arthur had had enough. He was depressed with what he saw on the voyage. The ports and natives were poverty stricken. The communities were in a shocking state of destitution,

most often struggling from disease and fearful for their lives. Where did someone find solace in a journey such as this? Alcohol was the option for too many, and even Arthur admitted that he found too much comfort in the bottle. Africa did not have the same appeal that the Arctic did.

And so, when the *Mayumba* returned to Liverpool, Arthur collected his wages and departed from the ship, never to return. His mother encouraged him to remain in the job for a few years, but he would not consider it. He felt he could earn the same wage from writing, and at least that way he would not suffer the terrific heat.

But another adventure was around the corner.

Budd and Arthur

Where was Arthur to go next? The young man seemed adrift and the family was concerned. After discussions with his mother and his disapproving uncles, he received a letter from an old friend, Doctor George Budd. Budd, already established in a successful practice in Plymouth requested that Arthur join him there at once if convenient, and if not to come all the same, to quote Sherlock Holmes. The family advised strongly against this.

But Arthur overcame his own reservations, and instead chose to envision opportunity and excitement. Doctor Budd had gained tremendous success with his medical practice, and wanted help from his old friend who he felt would benefit from the boom. Budd had previously fallen into serious financial issues, but while in Bristol he overcame all debt and apparently had prevailed as a successful doctor. Despite his reservations and Budd's unethical approach to medicine, Arthur took the plunge.

Doctor Budd was an eccentric, extroverted little man who at first brought colour into Arthur's life, and no doubt helped influence Arthur's writings. But he was the type of man who felt the effects of alcohol quickly, which only inflamed his expansive personality. He was also something of a ladies man, in the not so respectable way.

One particular occasion found Budd clambering out of a second floor window when the husband of the woman he was sleeping with returned home unexpectedly. Attraction to very young girls was another of Budd's indiscretions. In order to marry his wife, who was underage, he locked the girl's governess in a room, coloured the girls hair black, and the two eloped.

That was not the end of it. Doctor Budd's exploits could fill volumes of hilarious and unbelievable antics. And the contrast with Arthur could not have been greater.

On the professional side, Arthur had been promised 'all visiting, all surgery, all midwifery' and a 'guarantee' of £300 salary his first year. On his first day, Budd took him to the surgery and it was as described, crammed full of waiting patients! But Budd's treatment of his patients was something of a spectacle. He would yell at them and order them to be quiet whilst they sat in the waiting room. His insults were apparently what brought the patients in. While his consultations were free (the more likely reason his business took off) Budd was making his real money from over-priced prescriptions.

Arthur could not have been more different. As he began to see his own patients, his approach was in no way the same as Budd's. For one, Arthur would not insult them. As people responded to this and Arthur's portfolio of patients grew, Budd felt that Arthur was taking business away from him. Budd's attitude towards his old university friend grew from suspicious to openly hostile.

Budd took to snooping through Arthur's belongings and reading his letters to and from his mother, who was always very critical of Budd's methods. The situation escalated because patients were more keen to see a doctor who did not yell or insult them, and if they could not see the doctor they wished to see they would simply go elsewhere. Eventually, after ceaseless drama with Budd, Arthur took up a hammer, went outside and pried his nameplate off the front and cut his ties with Doctor Budd.

So where would young Arthur go next?

Portsmouth

June of 1882 found Arthur on a train bound for Portsmouth. It would be there, in this naval town, that he planned to set up his own practice, full of hope and imagining it flooded with patients, like Budd's surgery in Bristol. With his uncle's name as a reference, he was able to secure office space at 1 Bush Villas, Elm Grove, in neighbouring Southsea. Fixed to the side of the door was a brass plate engraved with the words 'Dr Conan Doyle, Physician and Surgeon' which he would polish at night under the cover of darkness, when no one could see.

July came but the patients did not. Many would stop and read his sign, but none entered. Finally one man did — but it was the local minister to ask if he would be attending the divine service that week. Arthur bluntly told the man he would not be attending and sent the priest on his way. What a disappointment.

Finances grew tight, and Arthur's brother Innes came down to live with him and help out at the surgery. This pleased Arthur who had found it too quiet and lonely. With the lack of patients he became well acquained with the local pawnbroker. He even traded medical services with other tradesmen which helped put food on the table. But boredom loomed. How to fill all this empty time?

His empty surgery left him plenty of time to write. He scribbled his stories and typed them up. And they begin to have success. He took his story *The Ghosts of Goresthorpe Grange* and sold it to the *London Society magazine* earning himself £10, which covered his first quarter's rent. He received another £10 for the story *Temple Bar*, and £10.10s for *The Captain of the Polestar*.

A number of magazines began to publish his work — *London Society, Harper's Weekly, All The Year Round* (originally founded by

Charles Dickens), and *Good Words* to name a few. For *Good Words* he wrote a science-fiction story titled *Life and Death in the Blood* in which a man is shrunk to one-thousandth of an inch and travels through another man's blood stream. While there is no direct connection, the concept of shrinking and travelling through the body was made hugely popular in the 1966 film *Fantastic Voyage*. More than anything it pleased Arthur to have the extra money while his practice was slow to take off.

"I polished my own plate every morning, brushed down my front, and kept the house reasonably clean."

By 1883, business began to pick up for Dr Conan Doyle. With sufficient funds coming in, he hired a housekeeper and Bush Villas was spruced up and looking good. Unlike Doctor Budd who had patients streaming in like animals onto Noah's Ark, eventually Arthur realised he needed to stop waiting and go out and get the patients himself. Church was out of the question for Arthur, so the next best way to get involved and meet others at the time was to join social clubs. First he joined the Bowling Club, then Cricket Club and the Portsmouth Literary and Scientific Society.

While he increased his social life to boost awareness of his medical practice he also persisted with his writing. 1883 also saw Arthur finally get published in the well paying *Cornhill Magazine*. His story *J. Habakuk Jephson's Statement* brought him 29 guineas, nearly half the year's rent! The success boosted the young Doctor's pride as an author. He could now think of himself as more than a 'hack writer.' Although after 'Habakuk' it would be some time before Arthur would see another success with *Cornhill*.

Arthur was amused by the stir his publications caused. When a man by the name of Mr Solly Flood read the story he foolishly mistook Arthur's story for fact rather than the fiction that it clearly was. Mr Flood made a point to correct Arthur's literary "crime" and informed readers that, 'Dr J. Habakuk Jephson's statement was a fabrication from beginning to end'. If nothing else, Arthur could lean back in his chair and smile knowing that his fiction was compelling enough to be taken as the truth by at least one gullible reader.

Arthur took up his pen again to write *The Narrative of John Smith*. Once completed, the manuscript was put in the post and sent for submission. For whatever reason fate was not working in Arthur's favour, and the manuscript was lost in the post. The manuscript did not surface until 2004 when it was purchased at an auction. It was then published by the British Library in 2011 and can be found in most major book stores. But it was not one of Arthur's strongest pieces of work. Arthur would later remark in the January 1893 edition of *The Idler*, "I must confess that my shock at its disappearance would be as nothing to my horror if it were suddenly to appear again—in print."

Arthur and Touie

A true romantic, Arthur always had an eye for the gentler sex no matter where he went. Between 1881-1882 he grew enamoured of a young woman named Elmo Welden. In a letter to his mother, Arthur made it clear he would marry her if he could. Elmo's £1,500 inheritance was much needed and he commented, "I wish her money was not tied up...If I could marry her it would fetch the practice up with no rush." However, after a trip to London the couple sadly parted, the reasons not fully known.

It did not take him long to bounce back. He wrote to sister Lottie saying, "I went to a ball the other night and by some mischance got as drunk as an owl. I have a dim recollection that I proposed to half the women in the room — married and single. I got a letter the next day signed 'Ruby,' and saying the writer had said 'yes' when she meant 'no'; but who the deuce she was or what she had said 'yes' about I can't conceive."

Romance aside, Arthur never stopped writing. In 1884 he worked on his second novel, *The Firm of Girdlestone*, a Dickens/Thackeray pastiche. By Christmas 1884 he published the *Crabbe's Practice in the Boy's Own Paper*. This story featured the first disguised appearance of Arthur's former University friend and eccentric employer Doctor Budd.

In March 1885 love would at last blossom for the young Doctor, coming as it did, paradoxically on the heels of tragedy. A certain Dr Pike called for the assistance of Dr Conan Doyle to consult regarding a patient named Jack Hawkins. Jack was suffering from cerebral meningitis and was terminally ill, both doctors knew. Mrs Hawkins, the boy's mother, was financially spent. She needed extra care for Jack but could not afford it. Arthur, taking pity upon the widowed woman and her family, offered to set up a room in his practice for Jack. Here Arthur was able to look after him carefully, but it was not long before the young man succumbed to his disease and died. Arthur was troubled by the death in his own house, and suffered along with the family. Mrs Hawkins was well aware of the difficult situation her son's passing had put Arthur in, for the boy's funeral was also held at Arthur's place. The affair become intimate and sympathetic.

" Touie "

One of the grieving family members was Jack's sister Louisa, or 'Touie' as she was known. Touie had blue-green eyes, curly brown hair and was a pleasant, round-faced woman skilled in needlework and piano. Arthur found himself calling upon her a few days after Jack's funeral to tend to her grief. After two months in each other's company Arthur was captured by her kindness, and her calm and gentle spirit. While Louisa may not have shared Arthur's craving for excitement, it is said that her sweet nature and unselfishness struck a chord in him, and by April the two were engaged. Arthur said of her, "No man could have had a more gentle and amiable life's companion."

However, before the couple's happy engagement Arthur received news that his father Charles Doyle had been arrested on charges of violence and damage and was soon sent to the Royal Lunatic Asylum at Montrose. There is no record that anyone in the family visited Charles. Though, for whatever reason, perhaps pity or sentiment, Arthur's sister Annette left instructions that upon her death her savings should go to her father. Arthur was less forgiving. He now made it clear that his mother was the only thing that would bring him North.

Over the summer Arthur applied himself diligently on his thesis for his M.D. Upon completion of it, and after the approval of his mother, Louisa Hawkins and Arthur Conan Doyle were finally married on August 6, 1885. The speed of their engagement and marriage raised a few eyebrows, though there was nothing scandalous about it.

Innes, Arthur's brother, was sent to Yorkshire for school, and Mrs Hawkins moved into Bush Villas with Arthur and Touie. At Arthur's inspiration, the couple enjoyed reading aloud to each other to help improve their minds. Arthur's practice was earning well enough to allow them to live comfortably and he did find marriage added to his waistline. One thing was clear, though.

The marriage brought a new happiness to the life of Arthur. Arthur continued to write and sent a story titled The *Firm of Girdlestone* to a publisher. Much to his disappointment it was sent back with a rejection slip. However, this led Arthur into his next breakthrough. Could he add something to the world of crime fiction?

The game was afoot, and something new was coming. A character named Sherrinford Holmes sprang to mind…but no, that didn't sound good enough! Arthur scribbled other names down. Finally he found the name that worked, a name which is known around the world to this day, and is often called the most popular fictional character of all time. However, it would be eighteen months before this new detective would meet the public in the novella *A Study In Scarlet*, but when the world met him it would never be the same.

The page from Conan Doyle's notebook, showing the alternative names for Sherlock Holmes and Dr. Watson, together with many other interesting memoranda.

Chapter 4

Mr Holmes, The White Company, Move to London

The Great Detective

Arthur spent six weeks writing a brand new story. This time he would venture into the world of crime. From Poe to Collins, detective stories had become hugely popular. People liked a good thrill, a good murder, a good chase! But what could Arthur add to this genre, if anything? He knew the tricks of Doctor Bell were something to behold. He also knew that this new detective could not just be smart, he needed to show his skills. If Bell could pull off such feats in the ward, it would not be hard to make the reading public believe it in fiction.

The story was originally titled *A Tangled Skein*, starring Sherrinford Holmes and his trusted colleague Ormond Sacker. Arthur felt that the new detective could not narrate his own exploits, "So he must have a common place comrade as a foil — an educated man of action who could both join in the exploits and narrate them." By the time the story was completed the title and characters were a little different. Arthur settled on a new title: *A Study in Scarlet*. His characters had a name change too. Sherrinford Holmes became Sherlock Holmes and for Ormond Sacker, Arthur chose a "drab, quiet name for this unostentatious man," Doctor John H. Watson.

It's believed that the name Sherlock was derived from two famous cricketers, T.F. Shacklock and Mordecai Sherwin. However, Arthur did have a classmate in Stonyhurst named Patrick Sherlock. As for the good Doctor Watson, it just so happens that there was a Doctor James Watson who was a fellow member of the Portsmouth Literary and Scientific Society. The true origins of these names are up for debate, but one thing remains: Arthur Conan Doyle had created an unstoppable crime fighting duo that would cause the public great joy but also personal annoyance for the author.

The story went out to several publishers. *Cornhill* rejected it, others returned it unread. Arthur wrote to his mother in despair wishing for his story to be picked up. But all good things come in time. *Ward, Lock & Co* accepted the manuscript under one condition, they would publish it the following year because "the market is flooded at present with cheap fiction". *Ward, Lock & Co* offered Arthur the sum of £25 for the copyright. He did not jump at the offer, the sum was not tremendous and the wait was quite long. In the end he agreed.

Surprisingly enough when *A Study in Scarlet* first appeared in *Beeton's* 1887 Christmas Annual no splash was made. Though the magazine flew off the shelf, and was sold out, reviewers didn't care to review a Christmas Annual. Imagine that,
what is now the world's most famous detective nearly slipped through the cracks!

Ward, Lock & Co weren't ready to leave the story behind either. They proposed a new edition be printed and the novel would be sold on its own. The publishers recommended Arthur's father, Charles, do new illustrations for the story. A man whose life had taken such a sad turn was thus able to battle back from his illness and help his son. I can only imagine the feelings Charles had during this time. Being relatively cut off from his family, he must certainly have felt proud to contribute to his son's literary success.

Many think piracy of creative content was born with the internet, but that isn't the case. When *A Study in Scarlet* was a hit in London it was pirated and soon enough found its way to America. To make matters all the more frustrating, at the time there were no copyright protection for foreign writers.

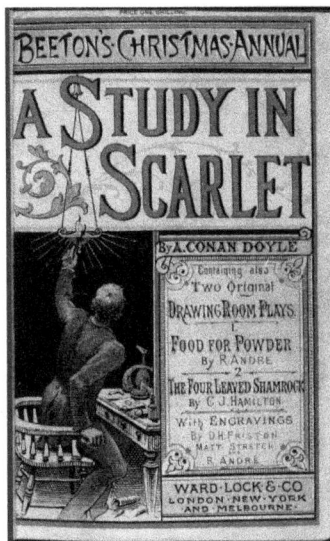

Joseph Bell was not the only influence for Sherlock Holmes, but where else did Arthur find his inspiration? One need look no further than Poe and Gaboriau. Arthur was a fan of both writers, and the techniques of Mr Sherlock Holmes were not far off from that of Poe's Dupin or Gaboriau's LaCoq. But he wanted Sherlock Holmes to feel more real, more scientific than other detectives who, in Scooby-Doo fashion at times, pulled the mask off at the end to reveal old man Withers was behind it all. In fact having Sherlock Holmes comment on Dupin and LaCoq as fictional characters was a brilliant way to establish Holmes as a real-life person. What better way to fool the readers, and though not by intent he knew he could, make the character as real as possible by commenting on current pop-culture.

Courtesy Toronto Public Library

Before *A Study in Scarlet* was published Arthur began work on another project that he was most excited for: *Micah Clarke*. The story would be a historical piece narrated in first person. Arthur believed that this book could "make" him as a writer. The story took place during the Monmouth Rebellion and blended fact and fiction. It wasn't until November 1888 that *Micah* would finally get its day. To Arthur's relief *Longmans* accepted the story. While Arthur awaited word on *Micah Clarke*, *A Study in Scarlet* was going for its second printing.

Between the acceptance of *Micah* and its publication, Arthur and Louisa were about to enter into a new phase in their lives together: parenthood. On January 28, 1889 Mary Louise Conan Doyle was born. The happy parents were greeted with more good news. Arthur's novel was a hit and was reprinted three times within ten months. Arthur was now successful as a doctor, a husband, a father, and a writer. It is no stretch to assume Touie was boastfully proud of her husband and the life they were building.

The Sign of Four

August 1889 saw Marshall Stoddart, the American publisher of *Lippincott's Magazine*, set foot in London looking for new writers. Arthur, along with Oscar Wilde, was invited to the Langham Hotel to dine with Mr Stoddart. He offered to pay the writers £100 each for a story no less than 40,000 words. From this meeting came two classics: The first was Mr Wilde's classic – the supernatural and intriguing *A Picture of Dorian Gray*, and Conan Doyle was inspired to write the second appearance of Mr Sherlock Holmes in *The Sign of Four*.

The Sign of Four only took Arthur two months to write. The story showed an incredibly detailed understanding of London, which was surprising given Arthur's limited knowledge of the city. So how did he create such a vivid picture of a city he did not know all that well? He admitted to Stoddart that he gathered his information from the use of a Post Office Map of London. Clearly, with a good map and a vivid imagination Arthur wrote, in this author's opinion, one of the best Sherlock Holmes mysteries—a dashing adventure, with a lost treasure, a subtle romance, and a boat chase on the Thames. The story further developed the characters of Holmes and Watson including Holmes's drug abuse and Watson's disdain for it.

It is really no surprise that Arthur allowed his impeccable detective to fall to the vice of drug abuse. He wanted Holmes to be vastly different from other fictional detectives, but also he wanted to keep as much space as possible between Sherlock Holmes and the blundering police officers of his day.

Oscar Wilde wrote to Arthur after he read *The Sign of Four*. Wilde wrote: "I am convinced that my own work lacks those two great qualities that your work possesses in so high a degree - the qualities of strength and sincerity. Between me and life there is a mist of words always:

THIS NUMBER CONTAINS

THE SIGN OF THE FOUR

By A. CONAN DOYLE

COMPLETE

FEBRUARY, 1890

LIPPINCOTT'S

MONTHLY MAGAZINE

CONTENTS

PRICE TWENTY-FIVE CENTS

J. B. LIPPINCOTT: CO. PHILADELPHIA;
LONDON: WARD, LOCK & CO.

Courtesy Toronto Public Library

I throw probability out of the window for the sake of a phrase, and the chance of an epigram makes me desert truth." Another reviewer said of *The Sign of Four*: "The best story I ever read in my life."

Perhaps one reason *The Sign of Four* was so quickly churned out, money concerns aside, was that Arthur was deep in research on something that had truly captured his passion. He was not at that time a strongly religious man (though he did explore Spiritualism later) but he had been attracted since childhood to honour, chivalry and heraldry.

All these would find expression on his next project as he immersed himself in the Middle Ages, preparing to write his epic novel set during those times: *The White Company*.

But sorrow befell Arthur and his family. As he completed work on *The Sign of Four* he received word that this sister, Annette, had died in Lisbon, at the age of only 33. Annette left her life savings of £420 to be used for the care of their father, Charles Doyle, who had been admitted into the lunatic asylum.

By July 1890 he had finished *The White Company*. But something caught his attention. Doctor Robert Knoch, known for his discovery of the microbial causes of anthrax, consumption (now known as tuberculosis), and cholera had made a wild claim that he had found a cure for tuberculosis.

Passionate and curious, yet unaware of how important this subject would later become to him personally, Arthur impetuously departed for Germany to see for himself if there was anything substantial to the Knoch's claims of a cure. But he had not secured a ticket to the lecture. Unable to meet with Knoch, or even gain entry to his lecture, Doyle resorted to looking over the notes of others who had the privilege of sitting in on the doctor's demonstration. From this, Doyle concluded that Knoch's

Courtesy Peter Harrington Rare Books, London

claim of a cure was premature.

On his way home he met Malcolm Morris, a skin specialist on Harley Street in London. Morris convinced Arthur that he should uproot himself from Portsmouth and move to London, assuring the young doctor that he'd still find time for writing but gain from the contacts and the extensive social life of The City. The specialty of ophthaology was broached. Arthur had some experience at the Portsmouth Eye Hospital.

But to specialise in London Arthur would first need more training. One thought was to go to study in Vienna, and then return to London to open a practice. When Arthur returned from Berlin he discussed it with Touie. Always supportive and encouraging, she agreed even though it meant leaving little Mary with Arthur's mother.

It was not completely without regret that the Conan Doyles left Southsea. He and Touie were much liked and would be greatly missed. By January 5, 1891, the couple took up residence in Madame Bomford, Universitaet Strasse 6, Vienna. Arthur continued to write during his time in Vienna. *The Doings of Raffles Haw* was Arthur's first commission while there. It was a short novella which he finished near the end of January, less than a month after arriving. Arthur admitted this work was not his best effort, but he was paid the handsome sum of £150. If anything, the story enabled him to pay his expenses.

Meanwhile, Arthur had also found himself a literary agent, the renowned A.P. Watt. This was a remarkable coup and Arthur was in good company. The agent's stable of writers included G.K. Chesterton, Charles Dickens, Thomas Hardy, H.G. Wells and P.G. Woodhouse. Watt was able to sell Arthur's short story called *The Voice of Science* to *The Strand Magazine*. Founded by George Newnes, The Strand would soon be ripe with fiction from Arthur.

After spending nearly four months in Vienna, Arthur was ready to return to London and

THE WHITE COMPANY

BY
A CONAN DOYLE
AUTHOR OF "MICAH CLARKE"

IN THREE VOLUMES

VOL. I

LONDON
SMITH, ELDER, & CO., 15 WATERLOO PLACE
1891

[All rights reserved]

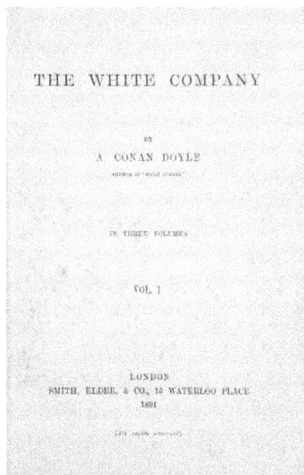

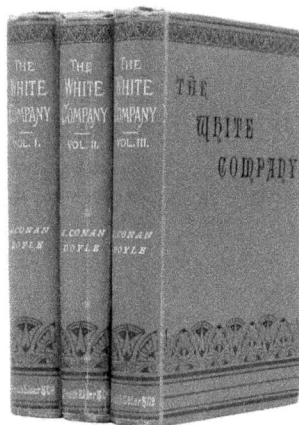

Courtesy Peter Harrington Rare Books, London

set up his practice as an ophthalmologist. The family moved into a residence at 23 Montague Place in Bloomsbury. With his family settled there, Arthur also rented rooms for his practice at 2 Upper Wimpole Street, not far from the famous Harley Street, where London's most expensive doctors practised.

Once again, Arthur found himself with time on his hands. New to the area, and with few connections, Arthur sat alone in his office. What was he to do with no patients walking through his door? He returned to a favoured project — his epic tale of the Middle Ages, *The White Company*. The story followed a group of bowmen led by the character of Sir Nigel Loring. The narrative took place at the time of the Hundred Years War during the reign of Edward III.

Arthur had researched his topic fully. He had read nearly 150 books on the varied subjects of archery lore, oaths, battle locations, training methods and details of the times. Arthur was something of a fanatic and deeply passionate about his subject. He channeled his love for chivalry and honour, instilled in him as a boy listening to his mother's stories.

He felt a great accomplishment and swelled with pride as he finally came to the end of *The White Company*. expressing his joy for the book and the characters to his family. He felt as if he knew Sir Nigel, Samkin, and Hordle. This excitement did not end there. He offered the story for serialisation in Blackwood's for a low sum of £300, believing it would do better to get the story into a good magazine for a smaller pay than to get better pay in a magazine less esteemed. But Blackwood's did not respond quick enough, and Cornhill bought the rights to *The White Company*.

In 1891the story was serialised before a three-volume novel was released. Considering the extreme amount of research Arthur put into his epic historical romance, he was deeply disappointed when reviews claimed the book was a thrilling adventure for boys with little or no remark to its historical importance.

"They treat it too much as a mere book of adventure," Doyle wrote to his mother. Despite Doyle's disappointment that the book wasn't heralded as a piece of great historical significance, it was nevertheless well received, and went through no less than fifty editions before his death.

Sherlock Holmes Takes A New Form

" Scandal in Bohemia "

Sherlock Holmes was about to make a dramatic return, not in a novella but in two short stories. With publications like *the Strand Magazine* and others offering both single and serialised stories, Arthur had an idea. The problem with serialised stories was this: if readers missed an issue they were behind and had to guess what happened. But, what if there was a series of one-off adventures with the same character? It would draw the readers to the magazine without fear of losing the plot.

Arthur submitted *A Scandal in Bohemia* which pitted Holmes against the brilliant adventuress, Irene Adler. She was quite the match for Sherlock Holmes. It was a bold move Arthur made, having Sherlock Holmes's third adventure be a loss. Not only was Sherlock Holmes outwitted, it was done so by a woman! Arthur's story elevated women in a time when they weren't always seen as equal to men. That alone was a brilliant piece of progressive and excellent writing.

Next came *The Red-Headed League*, a bizarre and comical story about a red-headed man named Jabez Wilson who was curiously hired to spend hours each day copying out the *Encyclopædia Britannica*. A story that started with Holmes and Watson laughing at the client suddenly became a thrilling and outstanding heist story. Arthur was able to blend the strange and outrageous only to quickly turn it around and make it believable and exciting.

These stories were illustrated by artist Sidney Paget. This artist was not first in line to do the illustrations. In fact *The Strand* editor, W. H. J. Boot wanted Walter Paget, Sidney's brother, who had done *Treasure Island* and *Robinson Crusoe*. By some happenstance the project fell to his brother Sidney, who was lesser known.

Sidney brought Sherlock Holmes, Doctor Watson and many more to life through his brilliantly clear and evocative illustrations. Sidney would often have people reenact the scenes that were to be illustrated, photographing them and sketching before going away to create the final masterpiece. The illustrations became synonymous with *The Strand Magazine*. But Walter Paget amusingly made an appearance; Sidney used his brother as the model for Sherlock Holmes. Walter, being a very good-looking man, was not entirely as Arthur envisioned Holmes. However, Arthur realised that a more handsome Sherlock Holmes would appeal more to his lady readers.

It's reported that Greenhough Smith, who read the handwritten manuscripts that Arthur submitted concluded Conan Doyle was the 'greatest short story writer since Edgar Allen Poe.' Arthur was then contracted to write four more Sherlock Holmes stories, offered at 30 guineas each. The six stories in total were all he planned to do with the great detective. Though *A Study in Scarlet* and *The Sign of Four* had previously been released, and received good reviews, it wasn't until *A Scandal in Bohemia* that the public became enthralled with the eccentric consulting detective who lived at 221B Baker Street. Now that the world had Holmes, they would never let him go.

The *Strand Magazine* asked for more stories beyond the six but having tired of the detective, Arthur refused. Meanwhile, his medical practice was doing poorly; not one single person stepped foot into his office. Clearly the bulk of his income had come from his pen rather than his practice. But before the fateful nail was sealed in the coffin of Arthur's medical practice he was stricken ill with influenza. It was no walk through the park to recovery. His sister, Annette, had recently died from it and he, too, was nearly claimed by it.

As it often happens when one recovers from serious illness, Doyle had the chance to reflect on his life and gain perspective on his true path. From his sickbed, Doyle wrote, "I saw how foolish I was to waste my literary earnings in keeping up an oculist's room in Wimpole Street, and I determined with a wild rush of joy to cut the painter and to trust forever to my power of writing. I remember my delight in taking the handkerchief which lay upon the coverlet in my enfeebled hand, and tossing it up to the ceiling in my exultation. I should at last be my own master. No longer would I have to conform to professional dress or try to please anyone else. I would be free to live how I liked and where I liked. It was one of the greatest moments of exultation in my life."

As soon as he was well, Arthur moved his family to 12 Tennison Road, South Norwood. It was June of 1891.

" Arthur & Touie Cycling in South Norwood "

Chapter 5

South Norwood, Switzerland, & Egypt

"Give us more Sherlock Holmes!" *The Strand Magazine* cried. It was October '91. *The White Company* was still in serial form with *Cornhill* with a single volume planned for the end of the year. Arthur was toying with another historical novel tentatively called *The Refugees* which would bring back Micah Clarke, this time placing him in the Canadian forests.

"More Holmes!" the Strand Magazine persistently asked. It was surprising that he could resist the hounding for more Sherlock Holmes, with his earnings from the detective being quite handsome. Writing to his mother Arthur said he would ask The Strand for a price so high they would likely come back and say, "Forget it." He asked for £50 per story no matter the length. Arthur waited for a letter in return saying, "The price is far too high." A letter came. He opened it, fully expecting a rejection. Unfolding the note, he began to read. His eyes widened, his chest raised, and he released a deep and exhausted sigh. To his astonishment, The Strand had agreed to his terms. By the end of October 1891 he had written two more stories: *The Adventure of the Blue Carbuncle*, the closest thing to a Sherlock Holmes Christmas Special; and

" The Boscombe Valley Mystery "

The Adventure of the Speckled Band.

Between July 1891 to June 1892 Sherlock Holmes was featured in every issue of The Strand Magazine. Holmes had become the Victorian equivalent of a superhero. Arthur ha====---d captured the imaginations of a vast readership. It became standard for people to queue in long lines at newsagents in order to grab a copy of *The Strand Magazine* – just to read the latest adventure of Sherlock Holmes!

The Victorian era was one of great scientific growth, and the character was a man of his times. Sherlock Holmes's love for scientific investigation captured the public imagination. London was also the political and economic centre of the world, which made the setting for Sherlock Holmes all the

" The Copper Beeches "

more enticing. Despite Arthur's limited time in London, his ability to bring it to life was remarkable and vivid, though he occasionally took liberties by inventing roads and place names, perhaps by artistic license.

Orson Wells later called Sherlock Holmes "the world's most famous man who never was." Arthur had created a sensation. People would go to Baker Street seeking 221B in the hopes of hiring Sherlock Holmes to solve their problem. Even to this day there are many people who believe Sherlock Holmes was real.

When the first twelve stories were completed they were compiled into one volume, *The Adventures of Sherlock Holmes*. Without doubt the book was a bestseller and praised by many, including the man whom Arthur based Sherlock Holmes on: Dr Joseph Bell.

Dr Bell wrote: "Dr Conan Doyle in this remarkable series of stories has proven himself a born story-teller. He has had the wit to devise excellent plots, interesting complications; he tells them in honest Saxon-English with directness and pith; and above all his other merits, his stories are absolutely free from padding. He knows how delicious brevity is and he has given us stories that we can read at a sitting between dinner and coffee, and we have not a chance to forget the beginning before we reach the end."

While it might not have been what he wanted, Arthur was becoming most famous for his Sherlock Holmes stories. It could be argued that his greatest strength as a writer was in his short stories, especially when it came to Sherlock Holmes.

During the boom of Sherlock Holmes, *The White Company* was still pressing on and Arthur was also hard at work on *The Refugees*. He had, however, decided against the use of Micah Clarke for the story. It was early in 1892 when *The Refugees* was finished and then serialised in the *Strand* before being released as a single volume. To Arthur's relief the story was praised. *Harper's New Monthly Magazine* called it 'A brilliant and fascinating story'. As much as the public admired his Sherlock Holmes stories, Arthur was very much in love with his historical pieces and desperately wanted his credits to be tied with them as opposed to silly detective stories.

During the excitement of finishing *The Refugees*, Arthur was invited by Jerome K. Jerome (editor of *The Idler* and author of *Three Men in a Boat*) to *The Idler's* dinner, one of the many literary parties at which Arthur found himself. It was here at the Idler's dinner he met J.M. Barrie (author of *Peter Pan)*. An easy friendship was struck between these men, especially for Conan Doyle and Barrie. At the time Barrie was working on the production of his first play titled *Walker*.

Arthur's own passion for theatre reignited at around this time. Adapting his short story *A Straggler of '15*, Arthur wrote the one-act play *Waterloo*. On a bold whim, he sent his one-act play to the famous actor and producer Henry Irving, whom he greatly admired. The anticipation must have been great as he waited to hear back. He received a letter almost immediately from Irving's secretary, none other than the future author of Dracula, Bram Stoker, saying that Irving had bought the rights to Waterloo. It was joyous news for Arthur.

He was in a writing frenzy now. He had promised a Napoleonic adventure for Arrowsmith titled *The Great Shadow*. *The Strand* came back again asking for even more Sherlock Holmes. But all the while, Arthur was desperate to focus on what he considered his more serious work, i.e. plays and historical fiction.

" *Arthur at work* "

He had already written to his mother while he was penning what became the Adventures of Sherlock Holmes to tell her that he might slay Mr Holmes at the end. His mother pleaded with him not to do something so absurd. Thus Holmes narrowly escaped death — at least for the time being.

The Strand now wanted 12 more stories. Thinking to quash The Strand's request, Arthur demanded the exorbitant fee of £1000 for 12 stories. To his shock, *The Strand* accepted.

One question will always be asked to a writer: What is your process? For Arthur this was a thorough and detailed affair. His process for mapping out a story followed as such: he would create the problem and the solution, because you always work backwards when telling a good mystery. Then he created an outline for the narrative, this helped to keep him on track and not lose where the story needed to go. He would also write detailed outlines about the characters, so he knew who was whom and what their personality was like.

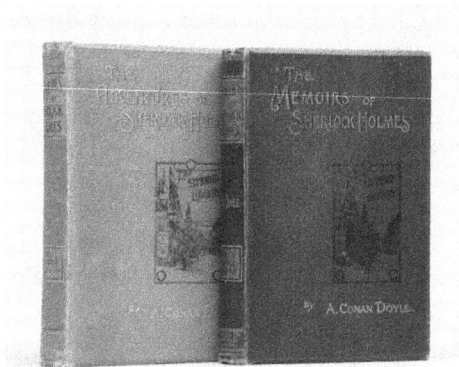

Many writers of today work in essentially the same fashion. He would work from a what is now called a "beat" or "step" outline and expand on each moment once that story arc had been completed.

Over his lifetime, Arthur was a remarkably prolific writer, whose output rarely wavered no matter what else was going on. He had set times that he would write, and discouraged all interruptions. His habit included two sessions per day; working from breakfast to lunch and then from 5pm to 8pm. He would write, on average, around 3000 words per day. That is, for any writer, a tremendous sum, considering he wrote by hand. This took a serious amount of dedication and focus.

Though he was churning out more Sherlock Holmes he made himself clear to *The Strand*: they could not expect the stories as swiftly because of his previous commitments, and as usual they agreed.

With the theatre bug itching Arthur, he pulled out a play that he had worked on during his time in Portsmouth. It was called *Angels of Darkness*, and was, interestingly enough, a recreation of the Utah scenes from *A Study in Scarlet*. Mr Sherlock Holmes is nowhere to be found in this play but Doctor John Watson is.

John Dickson Carr notes regarding the play: "Watson, in fact, once practised medicine in San Francisco. And his reticence can be understood; he acted discreditably." The play painted Watson as a womaniser and could have tarnished the stories Arthur was already releasing through *The Strand* should *Angels of Darkness* be released. He put the play away and at the time Carr was writing *The Life of Sir Arthur Conan Doyle*, the play had still not been released.

Touie, who was always a bit weak and

"Arthur Conan Doyle seated in the centre with his wife, Louise (Touie) to the left and his sister Connie to the right with her husband, E W Hornung, behind (1890s)"

unable to keep up with the fast pace of Arthur, especially when it came to their shared hobby of bicycling, was now pregnant with their second child. On November 15, 1892, Arthur Alleyne Kingsley was born. Finally, Arthur had a son. His love for chivalry was not lost on the boy, as he named him after a *White Company* character — Alleyne, the squire to Sir Nigel.

But still The Strand still wanted their Holmes. Reluctantly Arthur continued with more Sherlock Holmes stories. He was worried his second set of stories would not be as beloved as the first; and admitted as such in a letter to Doctor Joseph Bell, whom he had finally named publicly as the inspiration for the character of Sherlock Holmes.

The Silver Blaze, The Cardboard Box, and The Yellow Face had been completed. Doyle's worries that his new collection would be lacking were unfounded. The new stories were received with enthusiasm, particularly *The Silver Blaze*.[6]

Early in 1893 J.M. Barrie called upon Arthur for assistance. Barrie was working on the play titled Jane Annie - a comic opera. Arthur looked over the play and felt he could help his friend, whom he believed lacked the understanding of poetic rhyme. On May 13, 1893, at the Savoy, the opening night of Jane Annie saw both writers sitting together in a box itching with anticipation as they watched the crowds slowly enter and sit. The stage was set, the curtain rose, and they watched their play unfold.

But the unfolding, as it were, did not go according to plan. Jane Annie was a disaster. So despised by the opening night crowd (and later the critics) one of the actresses even refused to come out for the curtain call. A reaction like this would have shattered lesser men, but thankfully they were made of tough stuff. Both would later return to triumph.

But Arthur would soon escape England and put this one brief failure behind him.

Touie Falls Ill

Arthur was invited to Switzerland where, accompanied by Touie, he toured and lectured on 'Fiction as a Part of Literature'. Included on this trip was a visit to Meiringen, home of the Reichenbach Falls.

On his tour he met Silas Hocking, a United Methodist minister and author. Hocking later recounted that Arthur said to him that Sherlock Holmes *needed* to be killed off. "I intend to make

---

[6] *The Life of Sir Arthur Conan Doyle, Carr, p 70*

[7] *Author's Note: While not in mass production The Baker Street Journal does have the play available.*

an end of him. If I don't he'll make an end of me." The seed was planted, because there among the falls of the Reichenbach is where Holmes would eventually meet his nemesis and face a cold, swirling death. But before that fictional tragedy there would be cause for very real concern - Touie had fallen dangerously ill.

Coughing, endless coughing, and a stinging pain in her side. You can almost picture the concerned doctor and husband as he looked over his wife. Petting her head and holding her gently. He could not diagnose the problem; the matter was too close. This was not a random patient. It was his wife. He called for a doctor to see her. Though in other circumstances Arthur might have readily deduced the cause of her coughs and pains. The examination made it clear: she suffered from consumption, better known as tuberculosis.

Touie's family history was full of illness. Her father was diabetic, her brother and a sister both died young, and now Arthur's wife and mother of their two children was seriously ill. The doctor confirmed severe damage to her lungs which was unlikely to respond to treatment.

Arthur sought a second opinion from Sir Douglas Powell, a renowned consumption expert. The diagnosis was sadly confirmed. Powell said Touie might only have a few months to live. How could it be months? Arthur needed to find a way to save his Touie. Ironically, three years previously Arthur had travelled to Berlin to study tuberculosis yet he was not able to diagnosis Touie himself. Or perhaps could not face the truth.

What were Arthur and Touie to do? Would he lose his wife in just a few months? How would he maintain his family without his wife? She was his rock. He relied on her for much as he went on his adventures. Arthur wrote to his mother that Touie remained stable and hadn't lost much flesh, and on good days ventured out. What Touie needed, though, was a better climate, and her husband was prepared to give her exactly what she needed. This fight would not be easily lost.

Touie's illness would not be the only tragic news. In October 1893 word came to Arthur that his father Charles Doyle had died. Little time was devoted to grieving his father, as time was urgently needed to be spent ensuring Touie's recovery. Medical journals claimed the fresh air of the Swiss Alps could have rejuvenating effects on lungs. Thus plans were made to send Touie, accompanied by her older sister, Emily, to Davos to stay in the Kurthaus Hotel throughout the winter.

Arthur stayed behind to fulfil his contract with *The Strand*. Sherlock Holmes, now more than ever, had become a terrible burden for him. He wanted to spend time on serious work, not silly detective stories. Written in his "Ideas Book", that all savvy writers will keep, in December 1893 were two words: 'Killed Holmes'!

The Death of Sherlock Holmes

" Professor Moriarty in The Final Problem "

The world gasped as Sherlock Holmes and Professor Moriarty plummeted into the depths of the murky waters of the Reichenbach falls. The two men, the world's greatest detective and the Napoleon of crime would be forever locked in eternal combat in the swirling waters. There, Arthur would leave his creation to rest.

Arthur could not have anticipated the reaction the public would have to the death of Sherlock Holmes. The citizens of London mourned the death of Sherlock Holmes as if he was real flesh and blood. To many, the detective in *the Strand* had been real! Men wore crepe bands on their hats and black arm bands to honour of the memory of the great detective. For some it was an outrage, and they bombarded Arthur with letters of anger and abuse.

How could he kill Sherlock Holmes!

THE DEATH OF SHERLOCK HOLMES

The public outcry continued. The Strand lost around 20,000 subscribers with the death of this much loved character. The Strand went on to say, "Mr Doyle's feeling was that he did not desire Sherlock to outstay his welcome, and that the public had had enough of him. This is not our opinion, nor is it the opinion of the public; but it is, we regret to say, Mr Doyle's." One woman in an angry letter called Arthur a "brute". For Arthur, the falls of the Reichenbach were the perfect resting place for his character, "Even if I buried my banking account along with him," Arthur quipped. In 1896 Arthur told the Author's Club "if I had not killed him, he would certainly have killed me."

He cared little for the character and could not understand why the public were so in love with him. Sherlock Holmes adventures were far from serious writing, according to Arthur. They didn't have the depth or detail some of his other works possessed, or the academic merit, he thought. The real writing, the really good stuff that people should be concerned with, were stories like *The White Company*.

To Davos

Davos, in Switzerland, once an old farming settlement, had now become a popular and expensive health spa. Its visitors were mostly made up of deep-pocketed English families. Touie was receiving her treatment some 50,000 feet above sea-level in a valley situated between two snowy mountains. But her stay was costly. With Sherlock Holmes no longer an income for Arthur, he needed to get back to work. Arthur wrote a new book called *The Parasite* in 1894. But churning in his mind was a story that would explore the life of a young man in a way no other English writer had done previously.

That was the birth of a Brigadier.

By April that year Touie had improved greatly. She had lasted longer than the doctors thought and wasn't succumbing to her illness. In fact, she pleaded to visit England after several months in Switzerland. The fresh air and treatments were working, but both of them wondered if she should she risk venturing back to the toxic air? Arthur finally agreed that Touie could return if only for a few days, then she must come back to Switzerland.

All the while Arthur began work on *Round The Red Lamp: Being Facts and Fancies of Medical Life*. This new piece was a collection of mostly medical horror stories and not for the faint of heart. One story, *Lot No. 249* was about the purchase of a mummy and how it is brought to life to commit evil deeds. *The Doctors of Hoyland* was a unique tale about a doctor who set up a practice in a Hampshire village. When a rival doctor investigates this new doctor he is shocked to learn that the new doctor stealing his patients… is a woman!

This story is just one example which displayed Arthur Conan Doyle's sometimes progressive views on women and their place in society far from. In *A Scandal in Bohemia*, Arthur had no problem using a woman, the much admired Irene Adler "of dubious and questionable memory" to defeat Sherlock Holmes and nearly bring a kingdom to its knees. The portrayals of women in Arthur's stories varied greatly but he was clearly a strong admirer of the fair sex.

Touie's improved health was a relief. She was beating the odds and her stability reassured her husband while he continued his literary pursuits. An offer came to Arthur, one he previously considered: tour America and read selected pieces from his works. It was a brilliant idea, but could he really do it? Could he leave Touie? After his sister Lottie insisted he go, and Touie agreed with enthusiasm, his next thought was: 'who would accompany me?' That pin swiftly dropped on his brother, Innes.

More exciting news would come to Arthur. Henry Irving's summer season at the Lyceum with Faust was coming to an end and Irving planned to star as Corporal Gregory Brewster in Arthur's play *Waterloo*. It must have been a thrilling time for the doctor-writer!

America called. From October to December, Arthur and his brother travelled. From New York to Chicago they went, then on to Indianapolis, Cincinnati, Toledo, Detroit and Milwaukee. Arthur was exposed to all sorts of American ways, and made some interesting observations: "Americans could be well educated and have decent manners…and the women are not as attractive as he had been told."[8]

But distressing news would reach Arthur before he returned to Europe. While in New York he learned of the passing of Robert Lewis Stevenson. While Arthur had never met the man, Stevenson was one of his favourite authors and he felt a personal loss. Stevenson was also a fan of Arthur's, and now they would never meet.

Brigadier Gerard & The Inception of Undershaw

Arthur returned to Switzerland to the news that Touie's health had continued to improve. Thrilled by this, he was ready to take on a new challenge. Out of the depths of his imagination emerged a new character. Make way, for here comes Brigadier Gerard!

Gerard was a true Frenchmen. Doyle longed to write a special piece that took place during the Napoleonic campaigns. He had previously submerged himself in literature of the era, but felt it out of his power to reproduce anything of worth. But at long last, in the form of Brigadier

Gerard, Arthur fulfilled his wish. His first Brigadier story was written during the busy travels of his American tour, and by spring of 1895 he'd completed seven more.

And now, in the spring of 1895 a seed was planted inside Arthur that would soon give birth to a truly wonderful estate. During a quick trip to England Arthur met Grant Allen, a well-known author at the time for his works like *The Devil's Due and The Woman Who Did*. Grant Allen, like Touie, suffered from tuberculosis, but he managed to keep his illness at bay in the fresh crisp air of Surrey, in a place called Hindhead.

Both Arthur and Touie longed to be back in England. It was their home. Neither of them wanted to live in and out of hotels in Switzerland or Egypt. So Touie asked Arthur to investigate Hindhead, could it be a new destination for them? What Arthur saw was good. The air was said to be healthy, and this could help Touie. There was a community of creative people, which would benefit Arthur, and it was just far enough from London to be relaxing but not so far that Arthur couldn't go in regularly. Hindhead fitted the bill… and it would bring them back home.

But why buy a house? No, Arthur planned something better. He would build a house. One that would assist his wife, to make it easy for her to get around. He drew up the plans and handed them to his old friend Mr Ball. Arthur was told the new house would be ready in a year and left the men to work. In the meantime, he needed to keep busy until they moved in — and money needed to be earned to pay for this new home.

The Stark Munro Letters would be, Arthur hoped, his next great work. It was a somewhat autobiographical narrative in the form of a theological, philosophical comedy. "I cannot imagine what its value is. It will make a religious sensation if not literarily — possibly both. I really don't think a young man's life has been gone into so deeply in English Literature," Arthur wrote to his mother.

---

[8] *The Life of Sir Arthur Conan Doyle, Carr, p85*

The Stark Munro Letters tell a story of a young doctor, whose father is on death's door, but who must procure work in order to look after his family. The novel brought Arthur's old friend, Dr Budd back to life in the form of the character of James Cullingworth. Budd's eccentric actions and outlandish behaviour provided Arthur with a wealth of comedic material.

These humorous moments were intertwined with deep theological conversations, and the pondering of philosophical matters. Stark Munro brought events and friends of Arthur's to life — not only Dr Budd, but a young brother who came to live with him, and even a saintly mother figure.

In 1895 *The Stark Munro Letters* was published. But to Arthur's disappointment, the book received mixed reviews. For some the combination of humour, medicine, and religion did not strike a chord.

Meanwhile, work still continued on the Hindhead house. Remaining in Davos, throughout all her troubles, Touie was ever cheerful. She stayed at the hotel and continued to rest while her husband alternately worked hard, and sought adventure. Arthur was certain two more winters of fresh clean air would cure her. Her cheerful resilient spirit enabled Arthur to explore new things, and the new sport of skiing captured his fancy. He was determined to master it, and to introduce this sport to his countrymen, whom he felt would flock to Switzerland to enjoy and take on this thrilling challenge.

It was just as well, because they would not be moving back to England as quickly as originally planned. Their Hindhead mansion was still under construction in the winter of 1895 and would likely remain that way through most of 1896. The children, Kingsley and Mary were sent to stay with Mrs Hawkins while Arthur, Touie, and Lottie, his sister, toured Egypt.

The dry air of Egypt was good for Touie. During their stay she was well enough to join Arthur at many social events and take in local sights. Arthur and Lottie decided to climb the pyramids, something Arthur said he'd never do

DR. CONAN DOYLE ON "SKI."

again. Despite his willingness to make the ascent, Arthur was not a fan of giant three-sided triangles. He felt they were 'childish'.

The trio eventually made their way to Wadi Halfa in the Sudan. Their visit there inspired Arthur to write *The Tragedy of the Korosko*; a tale about a group of tourists who are assaulted by desert bandits. As Dickson Carr notes, Arthur's aim in for this story was to explore the characters: an Irish Catholic couple, an Anglican Colonel, a Presbyterian, and French agnostic.

By the time the Doyles returned to Cairo, war had been declared and Arthur noted: 'Egypt had suddenly become the storm centre of the world'. Arthur became a war-correspondent, but it was not safe for Touie to remain in the heat. Eager to get back to her children, Touie proved patient and remained ever supportive of Arthur as he embraced the exotic lifestyle of war-correspondent, a mission he promised would conclude by April. Arthur was disappointed to see no action during his time other than troop movements. Regretfully he concluded his mission and returned to Touie.

But Undershaw was still not finished, and the task had grown in scope. In early 1896, Arthur, Touie, and their two children Mary and Kingsley took up residence in Greyswood Beeches, in nearby Haslemere.

By the end of 1896 Arthur had published his coming of age tale, *Rodney Stone*, through serialisation in *The Strand* and then in full through Smith, Elder, & Co. Arthur was now charging *The Strand* no less than £100 per thousand words, a remarkable sum for the times.

Rodney Stone was met with some decent reviews but one critic, Max Beerbohm in the Saturday Review, ripped Conan Doyle apart for bad plotting and medical errors. Arthur did not take this quietly. He wrote to the magazine and expressed his disappointment that Mr Beerbohm had little knowledge of the era in which he was writing, and that certain points of his story could be authenticated. But this was not the last word, no! Beerbohm responded with a point by point piece on where Conan Doyle had got it wrong.

Battles with the press are rarely worth it, and eventually Arthur moved on. Wrong or not on certain points, the story brought him a grand total of £5,500. So in the battle of Beerbohm and Conan Doyle, it's clear who really won.

The end of 1896 came and with it a new horizon for Arthur and his family. Early in 1897, Arthur and the family would move once more before they took up permanent residence in their new home. For a short while they moved into the Moorlands, a boarding house in Hindhead. During the buildup for the family's move Arthur took up riding, but he never considered himself a great horseman. With summer coming to its end, the new house was ready to be furnished.

Undershaw was about to come alive.

Welcome Home to Undershaw

1897 was the Diamond Jubilee of Queen Victoria, who was the longest reigning monarch in British history until Queen Elizabeth II surpassed her in 2015. But 1897 was an explosion of celebration for the British Victorians.

This wasn't the only big event of the year. Arthur and his family were soon to move into their new Hindhead home, Undershaw. "It was a considerable mansion planned upon a large scale," Arthur remarked. The house stood just below an 895 foot summit on a four acre site. Arthur boasted to his mother that within a few years his investment in the mansion would be between £9-10,000, and that it was remarkable that he did not go into debt in the building of the house nor have to sell any of his shares.

Finally the beautiful, three story red-brick house with a long sloping drive leading to the front door and the magnificent views of rolling hills was complete.

"The new house, which I called Undershaw — a new word, I think, and yet one which described it exactly in good Anglo-Saxon, since it stood under a hanging grove of tree," wrote Arthur.

Undershaw had eleven comfortable bedrooms and dressing-rooms that could easily accommodate an array of guests. The drawing room, dining-room, and Arthur's study all benefited from the magnificent south-facing views. The grand entrance hall displayed swords and a spectacular stain-glassed window that was outfitted with family crests.

There are some interesting facts about this heralding display. Somehow Arthur managed to leave out a pictorial reference to the Foleys of Lismore. In a quick attempt to fix this error, he included a stained glass window over the main stairs that featured the Foley's crest. But then, in his haste Arthur managed to get the family motto wrong putting 'Patientia Vincit' meaning 'he conquers through bravery'.[9] The actual motto was 'Fortitudine Vincit' meaning 'he conquers through patience'. Or... maybe it wasn't a mistake, but a sentiment closer to his heart.

One can imagine Arthur walking through the house before anything had been moved in and before the family had seen it. Lovely dark wood floors would have greeted him as he opened the front door with its ornate brass handle and made his way into the grand entry with the stained glass glowing in the sunlight.

He might then step into lounge with its spectacular view of the Surrey hills, perhaps lingering to think about where he'd place things and how the house would be decorated for him and Touie. Beyond

'Arthur in his Study at Undershaw'

---

[9] Conan Doyle The Man Who Created Sherlock Holmes, Andrew Lycett, pg 240. Phoenix, London, 2008.

the lounge towards the Eastern end of the house would be his private study with a wine cellar. He'd place his desk in a pivotal spot to see outside, overlooking the tennis court, but also be able to happily greet those who entered the office.

The kitchen was ready and would soon be serving up warm meals for the family and guests. The ground floor with its lounge, sitting rooms and studies was spacious and inviting. Eloquently patterned tiles outlined many of the fireplaces, lavish wallpaper brightened the walls, and fine woodwork trim accented every room. Arthur must have been pleased as he ascended the stairs to the second floor. He and Touie had adjoining rooms. He would spend time with her, but let her rest in solace when she needed. Though both their rooms exited into the hall, they had a door which connected their two rooms for easy access. Arthur would never be far from her when he was home.

What a proud moment for Arthur, seeing what he had accomplished for his family. Seeing what he had done for his wife. Now it was time for them to move in. A second event marked this as a complex year for Arthur Conan Doyle. On March 15, 1897, he met Jean Leckie, the woman who would capture his heart and affection.

Touie was the mother of his children, the object of his care and devotion, indeed he had travelled the world in order to protect her health. As precipitous was his love for Jean, Arthur was a man of chivalry and honour. He had the deepest respect for Touie and vowed many times that he'd never hurt her, never be unfaithful to her; and in fact he remained true to her until the end of her life. But for Arthur, it was as if he were fighting the devil; like having temptation dangled before him like a carrot before a horse. To his credit, he fought the devil and won, as he would say, but it was no easy task and not everyone was pleased.

Arthur felt his feelings toward Jean were unfair to her; they were something he could not act upon. And he understood they were equally unfair towards Touie. Jean, however, cared not and was quite willing to put her own desires on hold, accept his admiration, and wait. It seemed she was willing to forever be admired by Arthur but never loved by him. Arthur was simply not willing to abandon, cheat on or divorce Touie.

1897 would begin a challenging period in the life of Arthur Conan Doyle.

The House and Grounds

Two years had passed since Arthur had bought the land for his Hindhead home. Finally he and his family moved in. October 1897, Arthur and his family finally occupied their new home: Undershaw. The total cost to build Undershaw was between extravagant sums of £8,000-10,000.

Arthur spared no expense to create this haven for Touie. Undershaw was the first house in the area to have its own power plant to sustain the electric lights. He spent around £550 for the power plant, £4,429 to construct the house, near £1000 to furnish it, plus smaller sums of £100 for the wine cellar and £80 for a table which he put in his private billiard-room. The mansion also included large living quarters for the servants, with their own private stairs to go up and down. There was a garage, stable, a coach-house, and a four-room lodge on the grounds.

With three peaks along the South facing side and many large windows to capture the light and scenic views of the Surrey hills, the grand red brick mansion was nestled perfectly into the hill. Despite its proximity to the main road, it was calm and quiet. On the southern side the grounds outside the house sloped. Amongst the vibrant green landscape which surrounded the house, there was a lush tennis court and further down, a deep and thick brush. To the left of the house stood a lodge and stables for six horses.

As you walked into the mansion and down a short hall, the focal point of the grand entrance hall was (and still is) a huge, stained-glass window depicting the family crests. To the left of the stained-glass marvel is a one of the three large rooms. The view from this room overlooks the drive and stable area. Going back through the entrance hall there were two other large rooms and a shallow stair leading to the second floor. Moving east you arrived at Arthur's study and the kitchen. Most of the rooms on the ground floor face south, looking over the valley. This included Arthur's study.

There was a piano in the drawing room for Touie, an upright Broadwood. The drawing room was adorned with various trophies of Arthur's and souvenirs from his travels.

Special design considerations were made for Touie, with wide and shallow steps to help her ascend the stairs with ease. Her comforts did not end there, she had a domestic staff

at her service, including a butler. In addition, Touie received help from her mother who now lived nearby.

Undershaw was a grand house and designed for entertaining. The history of Undershaw is filled with visits from notable writers, family members and friends. Arthur's brother Innes arrived in late October after the Doyles had moved in. His old South Norwood friend, Henry Buchanan came in November, and mid-November Arthur's Brother-in-law E. W. Hornung. Notably absent in those early weeks and months was Jean Leckie. In fact, it would be several years before she would sign the guest book.

Arthur believed he kept his deep affection for Jean private, and that his wife was unaware of his feelings for Jean. Was Touie aware that her husband's affections were being pulled elsewhere at this time? It is hard to say, but aware or not, Touie valiantly focused on the happiness of her children and husband, and on her own health.

Holmes and the Stage

Sherlock Holmes, Arthur's nemesis, who hounded him almost since the character's inception and even more so after he killed the character in 1893, now took centre stage. And it was with good reason, for no matter what he wrote, whatever new flights of fictional fancy came to Arthur, the public still clamoured for more Sherlock Holmes.

He was in no mood to revive the character, but he did have an idea: what if Sherlock Holmes returned to appear on the stage? Arthur's love of theatre was no secret, and perhaps Sherlock Holmes would be an easier sell than anything else. By the end of 1897 he had completed the script for a play called *Sherlock Holmes*.

If we suspect that it is only our modern media who obsess about the latest celebrity gossip we'd be wrong. Arthur had mentioned little about his Sherlock Holmes play, however, *The Northern Echo* somehow caught wind of the proposed play, and the papers were suddenly abuzz with talk of the return of Sherlock Holmes.

You can imagine Arthur sitting in his study and spitting out his morning coffee when he saw the headline! Had he mentioned the play too loudly, had a friend tried to cash in on the new story? But there was no evil deed at work, nor a mystery for Sherlock Holmes to solve. More importantly, this seems to have been by accident. Bless the excited mother chatting about her son's doings.

Arthur sent the play to *Herbert Beerbohm Tree*. Tree liked it and decided to take it on to showcase at *Her Majesty's Theatre*, London. Reports came that Sir Henry Irving would play the title character, but this proved to be false. Tree instead cast himself as Holmes, but decided he wanted to make serious changes and Arthur would not agree, therefore *Tree* withdrew from the play.

Sidney Paget, who had famously illustrated those iconic scenes of Sherlock Holmes for the *Strand Magazine*, came to visit Undershaw in December of '97. However he was not there to do more Sherlock Holmes illustrations. This time he was here to paint a portrait of the famous author. Paget was only at Undershaw a few days, where he spent a good portion of his time sketching Arthur.

By early 1898 Arthur had sent his play to Irving. He hoped Irving might take it on now that Tree had decided against it over creative differences. Tree's interpretation of Holmes would not be the one Doyle had written, and liking Holmes or not Arthur wanted his Sherlock Holmes on stage. When others 'suggest' changes to the work it can quickly put an artist off. Arthur felt the changes would make Holmes a different character than the one he had created, and contemplated setting the entire play aside for good. Eventually Irving, too, decided against the play. Bram Stoker, Irving's business manager, wrote in his biography on the famous actor that during the years 1898-99 Irving was ill and his stake in the Lyceum Theatre was under negotiation. So if Arthur was to put Holmes on stage it would need to be through another avenue.

Enter William Gillette. It was a curious event that connected the famous American actor with the famous author. It is said that a random American journalist from a 'no name' tabloid wrote an article in which Arthur Conan Doyle allegedly stated that Gillette should be the only man to bring Sherlock Holmes to life on stage. Though Arthur never said that, the article piqued the interest of Gillette when it finally fell into his lap and he asked to read the play.

Meanwhile, Arthur had written another mystery which was published in *the Strand* called *The Man with the Watches*. Though there is a 'well-known criminal investigator' in the story, it is not Sherlock Holmes, at least not explicitly. However, in the story the investigator fails to solve the crime, something that happens only rarely in the Holmes stories.

That said, it's not unlike Sherlock Holmes on occasion to be left unsure. Watson agreed the unsolved cases did humanise him, though Holmes would not consider them unsolved, but rather ongoing.

In June of 1898, *Smith, Elder & Co* published Arthur's book of verses: *Songs of Action*. The book explored many themes, some of which were of a difficult nature. One particular verse titled *The Passing* told the story of a man who committed suicide when confronted by the ghost of his former love.

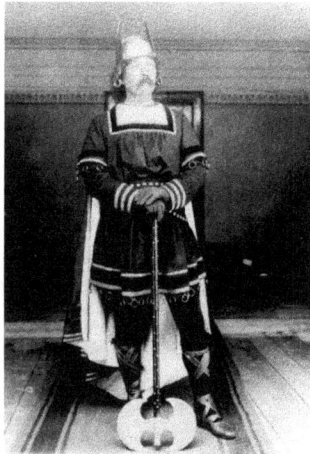

This was a hard subject for many members of the general public to swallow, and rightfully so. The verse seemed to favour suicide as a solution, which was, of course, illegal. It was simply highly disturbing to the reading public.

July was a flurry of excitement when both *The Era* and *The Daily News* reported that Arthur would be pressing on with his Sherlock Holmes play — now in collaboration with Mr William Gillette. In between the time he'd dealt with Irving and Beerbohm, Arthur had mellowed on the subject of making creative changes to the character. With Gillette, he took a much more relaxed approach on how Holmes was to be portrayed. The original issues with *Tree* were very similar to the changes Gillette now wanted to make to the character. But over time, Arthur had become open to them.

Arthur Conan Doyle dressed as a Viking for his fancy dress ball (23 December 1898

As the two men discussed what could be done with the character of Sherlock Holmes, Arthur finally said, "You may marry or murder or do what you like with him!"

Meanwhile, *The Strand* published a new short by Arthur titled: *The Lost Special* in their August edition. The story was about a railway train which disappears between two stations, and is said to be one of Arthur's finest mysteries. Though Sherlock Holmes and Doctor Watson are not named, the narrator is not dissimilar to dear Doctor Watson, and the amateur detective even goes so far as to say, "When the impossible has been eliminated, the residuum, however improbable, must contain the truth," a phase which echoes the nearly identical words Sherlock Holmes speaks in *The Sign of Four.*

November brought devastating news. Theatrical producer Charles Frohman's property had caught fire. One of the most tragic losses was the original manuscript of Sherlock Holmes that Arthur and Gillette had worked on. The entire property loss was estimated to be around $6,000.00. But for Arthur and William Gillette the matter was not all doom. Like all good writers, they had saved their notes. The story would need to be re-written, but not fully from scratch. Arthur would leave these re-writes to Gillette this time.

That autumn, Arthur was caught up in a new story. It was titled *The Duet* and concerned a couple named Maude Selby and Frank Crosse. This was a departure for Arthur, a domestic study which explored the inner workings of married life and the everyday adventures of wedded bliss. The humour and happenings throughout the book were honest and realistic for many couples. It did not resemble *Stark Munro* nor was it in any way autobiographical.

But to Arthur's disappointment, *The Duet* was met with mixed reviews, primarily because Arthur's fans did not expect him to write that kind of story. One critic, Dr. Robertson Nicoll, and Arthur had a very public disagreement about the book. Nicoll, who was not impressed with the work shared his review throughout several magazines under different names. Arthur quickly picked up on the trickery Nicoll was doing and called him out. Eventually the drama blew over and two men became good friends.

The Duet did have its fans, however. H. G. Wells wrote to him saying, "My wife, for whose verdict I waited has just finished the Duet….it occurred to me you'd not be offended if I wrote and told you we both liked it extremely." *The Duet* featured no murders, no epic battles or wars; it was just everyday life and how funny and odd it can be.

Sherlock Holmes Takes to the Stage

1899 began with William Gillette hard at work rewriting the Sherlock Holmes script. But it was not until May 1899 that Arthur would actually meet the actor. As the legend goes, Arthur was waiting for Gillette at the train station, and was baffled when Sherlock Holmes himself walked onto the platform instead. Mr Holmes (Gillette) approached Arthur, withdrew a magnifying glass and deduced that he was no doubt the author.

Gillette spent the weekend at Undershaw where the two men pored over the story. For copyright purposes the play was first performed at Duke of York's Theatre in London. This performance assured Arthur that Gillette was not going too wild with the character, and Arthur's letters to his mother and brother suggested how pleased he was with it.

Finally, on October 23, 1899, Sherlock Holmes starring William Gillette debuted at The Star Theatre in Buffalo, New York. The New York Times praised the play.

It toured, picking up momentum as it geared up for the important opening at the Garrick Theatre. After the that performance, Gillette gave a speech and laid any blame on the show on the playwright, which was him. The triumph of Sherlock Holmes was no doubt pleasing to the character's creator but also the actors involved. News spread about the play's success and Henry Irving stated that the play could open at the Lyceum the next spring.

"All seemed placid at this time. My wife was holding her own in winter as well as in summer. The two children, Mary and Kingsley, were passing through the various sweet phases of human development, and brought great happiness into our lives," Arthur wrote. However, there was more going on in the world at this point than family bliss and Sherlock Holmes. By now the world was two months into the Second Boer War; and this war would soon capture Arthur's attention.

The Boer War

Thirsty for adventure and the taste of war, Arthur jumped at the chance to volunteer when the Boer War broke out. It is the distance of history that now tells us that this was a war caused primarily by the discovery of one of a number of enormous gold fields. After Britain's humiliating defeat in the First Boer War, The Boers were able to separate themselves from British rule and set up their own state. It was only then that gold was found! And with this gold many British came racing to see what they had left behind. After unrest between the Boers and Britain, the Boer president Paul Kruger gave the final ultimatum that the British had two days to withdraw their soldiers. On the 12 of Oct 1899 war was declared.

Though his mother begged him not to go, Arthur was determined to serve. He had seen no combat in Egypt but was hoping to make it to the front lines this time. In addition to his spirit of adventure and deep patriotism, Arthur was also motivated to write a first hand account of a war. So he enlisted.

Deeply disappointed when he was told he was too old to be sent to the front lines. Arthur despaired, but hope was soon restored when he ran into John Langman. Langman was setting up a 100-bed hospital in South Africa and Arthur was invited to join them. While it wasn't front line action, it was a useful role and well suited to his talents. He believed this was a decent compromise to his mother's plea not to go at all.

He was clearly aware of the danger, however, as his preparations to leave included writing a final will and testament. Jean Leckie would not be among those to see Arthur off on his journey. The painful thought of a quick goodbye amongst the crowds of people was too much for her to endure. Later Arthur would learn that she was, indeed, among the crowds to watch the ship go off.

Arthur arrived for duty on the 2nd of April 1900 and joined Langman as the 'Secretary and Registrar' on the mission. He wouldn't be going on his own, a piece of Undershaw would come with him. Arthur took his butler Thomas Cleeve, a " good intelligent man." Mr Cleeve was a former military man and would have no trouble assisting. Arthur, went as an unpaid man on this Boer adventure, but he did pay Thomas out of his own pocket. Thomas Cleeve's wife, Elizabeth, who was also in Arthur's employ at Undershaw, remained at Hindhead. Both Touie and Elizabeth had no choice but to accept their husbands' call to duty.

As the time grew closer for Arthur to leave, Touie, who had been steadily improving, needed another boost of fresh air. She departed for Naples where Arthur hoped the warmer climate would

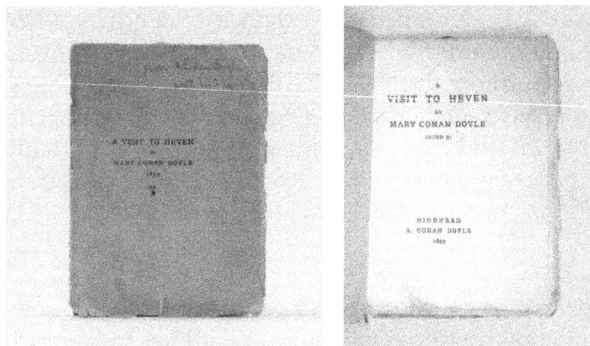

completely cure her.

While Arthur felt well fit for his task, he soon noticed that the leader of his unit was singularly unsuited. Dr O'Callaghan, a personal friend of Langman, was a gynaecologist, unfamiliar with the kind of wounds he encountered in a war zone, and was not apt to lead a surgery in the chaotic and stressful conditions. O'Callaghan eventually came to realise this and returned to England.

Though he was disappointed not to see action first hand, Arthur soon found that serving in the Langman Hospital was no easy task. Positive news was reported to the folks back home, but in reality the medical staff were overwhelmed and barely able to cope with massive numbers of sick and wounded. Arthur recalled attending a young, gravely wounded soldier. "Died as I fanned him. I saw the light go out of his eyes. Nothing can exceed the courage or the patience of Tommy."

During his service Arthur received a copy of his new collection of short stories called *The Green Flag*. The collection had been published in April and contained thirteen stories.

Arthur kept an extensive diary during his time in the war. He was critical of a number of British military practices. They made themselves vulnerable, he felt, by their antiquated weaponry and practices.

In the *British Medical Journal* Arthur wrote of many improvements which should be made including adding concealed weapons, a different deployment of observation-balloons, and getting rid of the cavalry swords, which, according to him, should be left in a museum. And finally, the infantry should dig trenches and not rely solely on the Sappers to get this done, as was the practice.

Arthur said, "The lesson of war, as I read it, is that it is better and cheaper for the country to have fewer soldiers who shall be very highly trained than many of mixed quality." This spawned the idea that Rifle Clubs should be started in England to help better train potential future soldiers.

From April to June Arthur served in the hospital, but by the end of June he was ready to return to England. It was on the return journey that Arthur met a man by the name of Fletcher Robinson. Robinson, (later the editor of Vanity Fair), was from Devonshire, near Dartmoor.

A born storyteller, Robinson regaled Doyle with legends and folk-tales inspired by his county and the mysterious moorlands. The two men became good friends on their journey home, and Arthur was entranced.

The hound was howling! One particular legend which Robinson shared was that of ghostly hounds said to be seen in the area. Arthur and Fletcher agreed they would meet up when back in England.

Return from War

Home at last, but not free from conflict. A worrisome and sharp enquiry on the hospital practices during the war forced Arthur to make a statement concerning the accusations of neglect. When interviewed by Lord Robert regarding several articles written by Burdett-Coutts cursing the state of affairs, Arthur was truthful. "Of course the state had in many cases, possibly in all, been awful, but the reason lay in the terrible and sudden emergency. Everyone had done his best to meet it and had met it to a surprising degree, but the cases of hardship were numerous all the same."

On the personal end, there was a sudden fallout between himself and his sister Connie and her husband Will Hornung. The root of this disagreement was Jean Leckie. Upon his return Arthur took Jean to a cricket match. Connie and Hornung felt it was inappropriate. But he felt he did nothing wrong by spending time with his friend. For Connie, she might have worried what Touie thought, or that Jean Leckie was now taking a higher priority in her brother's life.

To Arthur's relief, Touie's stay in Naples had improved her health, and they were able to remain at Undershaw. This allowed Arthur to pursue his cricket and hunting, but he was also burning to write about his time in the war.

He began work on his novel about the Boer War, but at this time suddenly decided to enter into the political arena as well by running for a seat in Parliament. With his background as a "historian" and his role in the South Africa, Arthur felt this would make him an ideal candidate for the Liberal Unionist Party in Central Edinburgh. When asked why he was running, he later admitted that he never had a truly intelligible answer. He had no burning desire to be in office, but in the case of the central Edinburgh his best reasoning was sentiment. Edinburgh was the city that helped make him.

It was a long shot, but Arthur had a lot going for him. Given his popularity as an author and his desire to engage in public issues he had a decent chance of winning the seat. Arthur could be found speaking from barrels or on pedestals, and hosting loud and uproarious meetings with the public about his campaign. However after a long battle against George Mackenzie Brown, he lost the seat by only 569 votes.

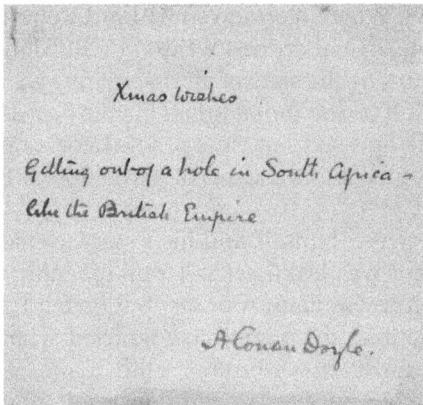

Arthur Sends A Christmas Card from War
Courtesy Peter Harrington Rare Books, London

Undaunted, he turned again to writing, and completed *The Great Boer War* by October 1900. It was published by Thomas Nelson & Sons, a thick tome of 552 pages. This was a remarkable accomplishment when one considers that he only returned from South Africa earlier that year and also ran for Parliament. The Boer War was arguably not a 'great' war in either size or impact, but Arthur felt he needed his book to have a title that separated this war from the first Boer War in 1881.

To Arthur's disappointment, *The Great Boer War* was considered too impressionistic and was disregarded as a genuine piece of military history. He went on to say, "No less than £27,000 was spent upon an Official History, but I cannot find that there was anything in it which I had not already chronicled, save those minute details of various forces which clog a narrative." Despite the lack of "official" sanction, Arthur used the book as a vehicle to express his wishes that the British Military would progress with their military tactics and step away from what he believed were outdated methods.

Undershaw Rifle Club & The Hound

Whether or not the British military were going to change their ways, Arthur took it upon himself to assist in the development of young men. At Undershaw he founded the Rifle Club. Meetings were held twice a week and Arthur would supply the men with weapons and ammunition. He hoped that in the coming years everyone in the village would be a trained marksman. His club did very well and grew to 300 members. Arthur believed a soldier did not need to be a 'specialised creature', but any brave man capable of holding a rifle straight would be a dangerous man. The Undershaw Rifle Club would be inspected by Lord Robert, who interviewed him after his return from the Boer War, and many other men of notability.

The way in which he ran the club was emulated by similar clubs, and with the First World War not far off, these types of clubs would prove useful for many young men. Soon many clubs had formed based on this model.

It was 1901 and Queen Victoria had recently passed away. Arthur joined his friend Fletcher Robinson, on a golfing holiday. This trip marked the start of something special. Writing to his mother, Arthur described a new story he was going to write with Robinson, and it was to be something frightful!

Later, speaking with Greenhough Smith, head of *The Strand*, Arthur requested £50 per thousand words for his new story and that Robinson would share a writing credit.

But the story began to change before Arthur and Robinson could begin work. A ghost from Arthur's past arose, once more, to make its presence felt.

For eight years the body of Holmes lay at the bottom of the Reichenbach Falls, but now, the ghost of Sherlock Holmes had risen. Having already made agreements with *The Strand*, Arthur wrote back to Greenhough and asked if the rate would be doubled if Sherlock Holmes became a key character for the story. With little thought The Strand agreed. The public was not finished with Holmes, they still wanted more, and more they were about to get.

Arthur and Robinson's collaboration would be short-lived. It's unclear why Robinson decided to back out of the project with his friend, but nevertheless he did. His influence, though, would remain. After all, had it not been for Robinson's stories Arthur might never have thought to write the chilling tale, thereby robbing the world of one the best gothic horror stories of all time.

The Hound of the Baskervilles would eventually be released in eight installments in The Strand between August 1901-April 1902. But in June of 1901, Arthur was staying at Morley's Hotel, Trafalgar Square, due to his cricket commitment at Lord's. During this stay Arthur wrote chapters Five and Six of *The Hound of the Baskervilles*. During these, Sir Henry Baskerville, is staying in the fictional Northumberland Hotel (set in the same area as Morley's), where he loses a shoe. It's no great stretch of the mind to assume Arthur based the Northumberland Hotel on Morley's. Aside from the Langham, Arthur used few real-life hotels of London in his Holmes stories. It's speculated that this is due to the fact that most hotels in Arthur's stories receive criticism, or are the scenes of crimes.

Further real-life events might have influenced Arthur. The two servants in the story, the Barrymores might very well be based on his own married servants, the Cleeve's. Mrs Cleeve's first name was Elizabeth and Mrs Barrymore's was Eliza. But also the Barrymores, in the story, are keen to leave Baskerville Hall. At the time of writing Mr. and Mrs. Cleeve were expecting a child and perhaps, it's speculated, that they, too, were considering leaving Undershaw.[10]

When, in March 1902, *The Hound of the Baskervilles* was released in hard copy, an article in the Daily Express said, 'Since the day when Dr Conan Doyle wrote *"The Final Problem"* and the waters of the mountain torrent closed over the head of Mr Sherlock Holmes, posterity has

"I SAW THE FIGURE OF A MAN UPON THE TOR."

confirmed the ruling which placed Sherlock Holmes as the greatest detective of whom we have recorded…Sherlock Holmes began life as a character in fiction. He then became a national institution. He may become a solar myth.'

How right they were. The legacy of Sherlock Holmes has grown over the years, to an extent Conan Doyle could barely have imagined.

But before *The Hound* was unleashed, there was Sherlock Holmes news elsewhere. William Gillette was in preparation to bring the play Sherlock Holmes to London in September. Following a huge success in America, it was anticipated to be a hit in London. When Gillette premiered the play it was well received with minor criticism that some members of the gallery could not hear the actors' voices, while some were confused by some Americanisms. Nevertheless the play was pleasing to viewers as it touched upon various plots from the original stories as Sherlock Holmes battled Professor Moriarty. The run ended in April 1902, after a remarkable 216 performances. That same month the final installment of *The Hound of the Baskervilles* was released.

While *Sherlock Holmes the play* and *The Hound of the Baskervilles* were captivating the general public, Arthur was still having issues at home. His sister Connie continued to voice her disapproval about his relationship with Jean. Arthur's mother tried to soothe things between the siblings, and Arthur, too, attempted to reconcile with everyone. Arthur felt his friendship with Jean was safe and no wrong was being done. They were friends and nothing more.

In early 1902 he decided to visit his sister Ida and her husband on Gaiola. Arthur was accompanied by Jean to the ship which would take him away. Arthur wrote to his mother to say that it was 'quite safe' and nothing untoward happened. However, he also recounted to his mother that Jean decorated his room with flowers and kissed his pillow. Clearly theirs was more than a casual friendship and yet many feel that Arthur continually took

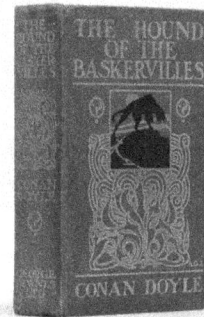

Courtesy Peter Harrington Rare Books, London

the high road in spite of his feelings and remained true to Touie. But obviously this came at a tremendous cost.

Knighthood

1902 was the year Arthur Conan Doyle would be offered a knighthood, and it was also the year he nearly refused it. When more allegations of misconduct surfaced about the British Military's actions during the Boer War, Arthur wrote a piece called *The War in South Africa: Its Cause and Conduct*. This was published by *Smith, Elder & Co* in January 1902. It picked up momentum and by February was being translated and being made ready for other countries. It was the success of this book that sparked the idea of honouring Arthur, but he frowned upon the idea of a knighthood.

Arthur gave credit to Jean for this book, later saying, "It is a high and heaven-sent thing, this love of ours. First A Duet and then this Pamphlet have come straight from it. It has kept my soul and emotions alive." Arthur further wrote to his mother saying, "It was kind of you, Ma'am, to write Jean such a letter and offer her Aunt Annette's bangle. I always feel that Aunt Annette knows and approves of our love. We often have that sense of a Guardian Spirit." Arthur truly found himself in a difficult position.

His love for Touie never diminished. Everything he'd done had been for her, moving to Switzerland and doing his best to constantly provide for her and the children including building Undershaw for her. But he struggled with the fact she was too unwell to be social and go out and have adventures, and Arthur, it seems, felt he found a fellow adventurer in Jean.

The questions of honours troubled Arthur. He said he valued the title of Doctor more than any royal decorations. In early 1902, he had already been to invited to a Royal dinner party based on the success of his war pamphlet, and had even sat next to the King. But he wrote to his mother that he did not wish a Knighthood.
Said he: "It is a silently understood thing in this world that the big men - outside diplomacy and the army, where it is a sort of professional badge - do not condescend to such things. Not that I am a big man, but something inside me revolts at the thought…All my work for the State would seem

tainted if I took a so called 'reward'."

His mother did not agree, and sent him a flood of letters telling him so. Soon enough he would not be able to hide behind the pen. Little Mary Doyle arrived at Undershaw and the matter would be settled. "Has it not occurred to you that to refuse a knighthood would be an insult to the King?" she said to him.

"I tell you Ma'am, I can't do it! As a matter of principle!" he returned.

"If you wish to show your principle by an insult to the king, no doubt you can't."

His mother won. Arthur's name appeared in the Honours list to be awarded on the 26th of June 1902, but two days before this, the King fell ill, and the ceremony was moved to October of that year. It is no coincidence that when Arthur came to write the Sherlock Holmes adventure *The Three Garridebs*, a story in which Sherlock Holmes refuses a knighthood, the date fell upon June 26th.

Arthur wrote to his brother Innes saying, "I feel like a new married girl who isn't sure of her own name. They also made me Deputy-Lieutenant of Surrey, whatever that means." If there was ever a moment where Arthur was acting like Sherlock Holmes it was here. His blasé attitude toward the titles is both shocking and humorous. It's no wonder it ended up in one of Arthur's later Sherlock Holmes mysteries.

October 24th was the fateful day when he accepted a knighthood and became Sir Arthur Conan Doyle. Strangely, Arthur's mother was not in attendance. However, Touie and the children and the Hornungs and Angells were there. Given that it was Arthur's mother who was so passionate about his acceptance of the title, her absence from the ceremony is a puzzle.

November saw younger brother Innes return from South Africa after four years of service. Innes was greeted by Arthur, their mother, and Connie. Taking a train from Waterloo they went to Haselmere, the closest station to Undershaw. After a long procession from Haslemere to Hindhead there was a huge party held at Undershaw. The lawn was decorated with fairy lamps and Chinese lanterns. It is a beautiful sight to imagine.

Arthur's New Toy

Before the end of 1902 Arthur had begun work on Adventures of Gerard, his second volume of stories featuring the Brigadier. Arthur loved the Napoleonic era and was more than happy to return to it. By spring of 1903 the collection was complete.

---

[10] *An Entirely New Country, Duncan, p148*

One thing continued to nag him: *The Hound of the Baskervilles* was a smash hit and the public's hunger for more Sherlock Holmes only intensified. Why couldn't Arthur reach into the watery abyss and rescue the famous detective?

But a new distraction arose… perhaps. There was clearly a distraction, other than the fact he probably just didn't want to focus on Holmes. News in Hindhead got around that Arthur had bought himself a new toy. It was on four wheels and powered by an engine.

It must have come as a shock for the horses in Undershaw's stable to see a brand new motor-car parked next to them! Purchased in Birmingham, Arthur had bought a ten-horse-powered Wolsley. Five could sit comfortably, seven could be squashed in if need be. When the car was ready to be picked up Arthur decided to drive it himself from Birmingham to Hindhead, around 150miles. Given that Arthur was little used to driving, a trip of this length seemed a little mad. Even Innes begged Arthur to be careful on his long journey from the midlands.

Crowds gathered back home to await his approach. The dark blue car and red wheels streaked down the roads like a lightning bolt as he approached Undershaw. With a roar of the engine and the popping of rock beneath the wheels he barrelled down the path and pulled the car to a swift and sudden stop outside Undershaw's front door. How pleased Arthur must have been with his new toy.

One can imagine him stepping out of the motor-car while the dust continued to settle, standing back to admire his shiny new acquisiton, arms akimbo. Perhaps he gave a few soft kicks on the front tire then turned to look at Touie, who, standing silhouetted in the front door of Undershaw, smiled indulgently at him. "Not bad, that," said Arthur, reflecting her smile.

Holmes, You Are Alive!

Collier's Weekly came knocking. They couldn't wait any longer. The world needed Sherlock Holmes and they were willing to pay the price. Mr Hapgood, the new editor of the magazine showed his "stellar" negotiating skills by offering Arthur £6k -- to which Arthur, an increasingly savvy negotiator himself, responded with a counter offer: the same fee, but for the American rights only.

Hapgood was desperate. The world needed Sherlock Holmes! He offered Arthur, in American dollars, the outstanding sum of $25k for six stories, $30k for eight stories, or $45k for thirteen stories, and this was solely for the American rights …plus the story length was not specified. George Newnes at *The Strand Magazine* was then willing to pay £100 per thousand words for the British rights to any new Holmes stories.

Arthur would have had to have been a madman not to accept the offer. With no set word-limit for the stories Arthur would net a serious sum of money for a collection he could easily write in a few weeks' time. How could he resist? Arthur replied to his agent regarding the contract by simply saying, "Very well, A.C.D."

It is perhaps ironic that Arthur's mother would show some concern about his decision to bring Holmes back to life. Her worry was that forcing more Sherlock Holmes for the sake of a nice pay cheque might result in poorly written stories. Innes, however, was thrilled when he learned of Sherlock's return saying, "Good old Sherlock. I think he has had quite a long enough rest."

"I might add" Arthur wrote to his mother, "that I have finished the first one, called The Adventure of the Empty House. The plot, by the way, was given to me by Jean; and it is a rare good one. You will find that Holmes was never dead, and that he is now very much alive." In Oct 1903 *The Empty House* was released. Newsstands, libraries, railway bookstalls were all bombarded with excited customers ready to read about the return of Sherlock Holmes. The public would learn that Sherlock Holmes was able to thwart the fiendish Professor Moriarty using a Japanese fighting technique

called "baritsu". It is likely Arthur meant bartitsu, a fighting style invented by Edward Barton-Wright, and a kind of English martial art of self-defence with a walking stick, but incorporating jujitsu, and western fighting.

In any case, Holmes sent the villain over the edge and to his death. Watson would learn that Sherlock Holmes faked his death in order to have the freedom to hunt down the rest of Moriarty's criminal colleagues and break down the empire he created.

Arthur followed *The Adventure of the Empty House* with *The Norwood Builder, The Dancing Men,* and then *The Solitary Cyclist*. Greenhough Smith gave Arthur come criticism on *The Norwood Builder* and *The Solitary Cyclist*. Neither story featured a shocking crime, and Greenhough wanted stories that would shock.

Arthur did try and re-work *Solitary Cyclist* but in the end was not able to justify changing it to fit Greenhough's wishes as the story was already a good one. *The Return of Sherlock Holmes* ultimately concluded with the thrilling tale, *The Adventure of the Second Stain* which features some of Holmes' finest deductions.

Arthur set the new stories between the years 1894-1898. He didn't want to suddenly throw Holmes into a contemporary setting. Sherlock Holmes and Doctor Watson were products of the Victorian Era and should, for now, remain there. Arthur didn't want to throw them into a buzzing world with telephones, motor-cars, and the like.

Jean's influence on the new set of stories reached beyond *The Empty House*. The 6th story written by Arthur titled *Black Peter* was set in Sussex in Forest Row. This was not a great distance from Ashdown Park Hotel where Arthur had been in 1901 during the census, with Jean. Jean's family were also from Blackheath, the

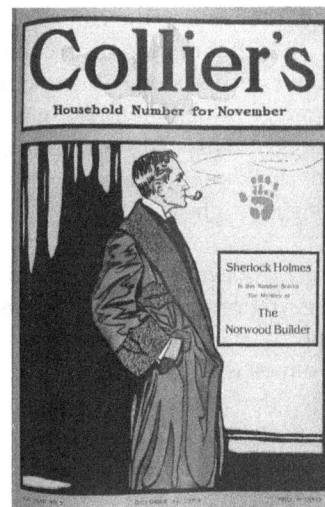

same area that, in *The Norwood Builder*, the character John Hector MacFarlane was from.

A concern Arthur had when writing the new Sherlock Holmes stories was the problem of similarity. He found it hard to come up with new and exciting, bizarre cases and brilliant deduction — a problem many crime writers have! He found inspiration anywhere and everywhere. *The Priory School* was inspired by an inscription from a counterfeit horseshoe. *The Dancing Men* was inspired by the young son of a landlord who drew stickmen. Struggling or not, Arthur was still cracking out stellar mysteries that were never lacking in imagination.

Touie, The Family Rock

Family life was different these days at Undershaw. Mary who, as a toddler, had crawled upon Arthur's desk while he wrote the Adventures of Sherlock Holmes, was now a young woman. By this point she and her brother Kingsley had learned to tread lightly around their father. While Arthur took great pleasure in jaunting about and laughing with the adults, he could by contrast be quite stern with his children. His temper would rage if they forgot to tell him something. They were also under strict instructions to make no noise while he wrote. Arthur, to his children, had become a stranger with an unpredictable nature.

By contrast, and despite her illness, Touie remained cheerful and was of great comfort to the children. On her good days she would go out in the carriage, often accompanied by her mother. But sadly her health continued to decline. She was ever the fighter, though.

Perhaps it was guilt that drove him, but when Arthur was away (even on excursions with Jean) he would always return with a gift for Touie. He once brought back a diamond bracelet and a card on which was written: "Here's brightness for your wrist dear wife, but you put brightness in all my life."

Meanwhile Jean was becoming more and more a part of the family. Lottie, Arthur's sister, was in regular contact with Jean. Arthur's mother was complicit in keeping the relationship under wraps. On March 16, 1904, Arthur wrote to his mother about Jean, "I brought Billy" (Arthur's nickname for his motor-car) "up as far as Surbiton and we celebrated J's fete day (birthday) by a drive and a pleasant day in the open. We have been together seven years from yesterday now, and our love has grown with the years. We have had our shadows - caused by the intensity of our love and our most difficult position, which nothing but the most determined courage could overcome, but no man could have had a more tender and loving helpmate, nor one who really did help him more when it came to practical things."

Later in March, Arthur and Innes took the car out for a drive. Driving was one of his greatest pleasures. As he pulled into Undershaw, travelling fast as he liked to do, he hit the gate which sent the car spinning and toppling over, trapping Arthur and Innes underneath it. Both men were most fortunate to walk away with but a few bruises. This wouldn't be the last time Arthur's need for speed would see him and his motor-car in trouble. For now, both Arthur and Innes were simply happy to have survived a crash that very nearly could have killed them both.

Sherlock Holmes and Undershaw

Arthur had made a promise to *McClure's Magazine* for a Sherlock Holmes story. He began work on one of his longest short stories, *The Adventure of the Second Stain*. When completed, it numbered 10,000 words. *The Priory School* was the longest, being over 11,000 words. Previously most of Arthur's Sherlock Holmes short stories were around 8,000-9,000 in length. When the story was presented and the cost of securing rights McClure's decided not to accept the story. It must have been slightly disappointing for Arthur for them not to take it, but *The Strand* and *Collier's* were happy to accept it.

The Adventure of the Second Stain would be the final Sherlock Holmes adventure that Arthur would write at Undershaw. No doubt the Undershaw years produced some of the finest Sherlock Holmes stories including gothic horror *The Hound of the Baskervilles*, Sherlock Holmes resurrection in *The Empty House*, and the thrilling battle between the great detective and the master blackmailer in *Charles Augustus Milverton*.

Family photograph At Undershaw

In 1904 Arthur helped found the *Hindhead Golf Club*. In early 1905 he was elected president of the club, but the organisation struggled financially and several members were forced to loan the club money in order to see the Golf Course completed, 7 of the 18 holes were all that was completed; Arthur didn't contribute a vast amount, only £100. There was no reason for him to take a big financial loss for the club.

In April he was awarded an honorary doctorate of law by his alma mater, Edinburgh University. Unlike his previous 'honours' this one he was happy to receive.

September 1905 saw William Gillette return to London. When the original run of Sherlock Holmes came to an end in London it did a final tour. A young actor by the name of Charlie Chaplin was cast as Billy the pageboy. Gillette was in London at Duke of York's Theatre with the play *Clarice*. Gillette had penned a short one-act opener titled *The Painful Predicament of Sherlock Holmes*. Charlie Chaplin was cast, again, as the pageboy.

Unfortunately Gillette's play, *Clarice*, was a disaster. The doors closed in October the same year. Gillette had to move quickly in order to rescue the season, and who better to save the day than Sherlock Holmes! The 17th saw the revival of Sherlock Holmes after 6 years since the play finished. Charlie Chaplin was hired to play Billy the pageboy for the run.

Sir Nigel

Arthur tried his hand as a playwright, and unfortunately it was never anything that really took off. Yes, Sherlock Holmes was a success, but even he gave credit to William Gillette for that. In November the New York Times interviewed him at Undershaw to discuss his attempt at play writing. The article was called *Conan Doyle's Hard Luck as a Playwright*.

In the interview Arthur mentions the trouble he had at finding a theatre manager to take

Arthur on a bike

on his play based on Brigadier Gerard. Arthur said, "I have offered it to nearly every London manager, but without success. They all seem to fight shy of it. Why, I cannot say. I am still confident, however, that it is a good play, and they," he added with a laugh, "are equally certain that it is not"

During the interview he also mentioned something he was eager to work on, a prelude to *The White Company*. Arthur believed that going back and telling a story that pre-dated the first was a unique and original approach to storytelling. The "prequel" is now almost standard in modern entertainment and has been used in a host of franchises from *Star Wars* to *Harry Potter*. Arthur said, "Why am I going back this way? Because I am tired of Sherlock Holmes. I want to do more solid work again. Sherlock and Gerard are alright in their own way, but, after all, one gets very little satisfaction from such work afterwards."

Sir Nigel would be the prelude to *The White Company* and would commence serialisation in December in The Strand Magazine. Sir Nigel himself had been a leading character in *The White Company*, but the connection was not overtly stated.

To Arthur's dismay, critics saw *Sir Nigel* as another boys' adventure tale as opposed to the "high-water mark in literature" that he felt it was. One reviewer commented, "There is nothing novel or ambitious about the book; this kind of work has been done before, though rarely with such spirit and gusto as Sir Arthur Conan Doyle brings to the task…it is like a breath of fresh air to find ourselves once more in the open, riding side by side with these simple hearted knights…Sir Nigel is the boys' book of the year." Hardly harsh words, but nevertheless not what he had hoped.

The Descent

By the end of December grief would befall the family when Touie's mother, Emily Hawkins, passed away. Her funeral was front page news mainly due to the fact a motor-car was used as a hearse, a novelty in those days.

Emily Hawkins had been a godsend for Arthur and Touie. She was always on the ready to look after the children when Arthur wanted to go to Europe for further medical study in 1891 and again in 1893 while Touie battled her illness. Her loss naturally hit Touie quite hard.

The beginning of 1906 was further darkened by grief, and by Spring Touie's health had declined precipitously. The tuberculosis had now spread into her throat, meaning she could only speak in whispers. The strong-willed woman that she was remained cheerful for her children.

Mary would later recall, "There was still the brave, gay little smile…Never a word of complaint. Her only thought was for our happiness." Mary also recalled a conversation between herself and Touie regarding marriage. Touie knew Arthur's heart lay with Jean. She told Mary that she should not be surprised if her father should remarry; Touie added that a new marriage would be given her blessing.

All was exposed when Touie told Mary that Jean Leckie would likely be her step-mother. Throughout Arthur and Jean's relationship there is no evidence that Touie hinted at her knowledge of it. But what she told to 17-year- old Mary was proof that, for all the games the family played, Arthur's feelings were known.

A glimmer of hope returned when Touie was well enough to go with Innes to the theatre in London in June, but that glimmer would quickly fade. By the end of June things took a terrible turn. Arthur was continuously keeping Innes up-to-date with one liners about her state. "Dear chap," Arthur wrote to Innes, "It may be days, or it may be weeks, but the end now seems inevitable… she is painless in body, and easy in mind, taking it all with the usual sweet and gentle equanimity." With the end in sight Mary and Kingsley were rushed home from boarding school.

When the time for final goodbyes came Mary recalled, "When the sad hour of parting came my father sat by the bedside, tears coursing down his rugged face, and her small white hand enfolded in his huge grasp. As I bent down to kiss her she murmured 'Take care of Kingsley; and soon after her lovely spirit passed away."

---

[11] *A Life In Letters: Arthur Conan Doyle, Edited by Jon Lellenbergz, Daniel Stashower & Charles Foley. Harper Perennial, 2007, p 552.*

July 4, 1906, at 3am Lady Louisa (Touie) Conan Doyle parted from her family. She was 49 years old. She had battled valiantly against her illness, and Arthur, despite his struggles, did his best to provide for her and support her health. Arthur went on to say, "Her end was painless and serene. The long fight had ended at last in defeat, but at least we had held the vital fort for thirteen years after every expert had said that it was untenable."

This was true, she remained with her family much longer than many would have expected. Dr Dalton gave her a few months to live but survived for an additional thirteen years, and she left behind a beautiful legacy of two children. In Arthur's autobiography Touie's death is but one short paragraph, but his words are powerful and capture his love and care for her, and he does admit to days of darkness after her passing.

However, he says more about her earlier on in his autobiography. "Our union was marred by the sad ailment which came after a few years to cast its shadow over our lives, but it comforts me to think that during the time when we were together there was no single occasion when our affection was disturbed by any serious breach or division, the credit of which lies entirely with her own quiet philosophy, which enabled her to bear with smiling patience not only her own sad illness, which lasted so long, but all those other vicissitudes which life brings with it. I rejoice to think that though she married a penniless doctor, she was spared long enough to fully appreciate the pleasure and the material comforts which worldly success was able to bring us."

Touie was buried in St Luke's Churchyard, Grayshott, Hindhead, with a large marble cross as the marker. At a much later date she would be joined by both Mary and Kingsley.

While Arthur fell into a dark place after Touie's passing, Innes' diary tells us a little more about what Arthur did during those days which followed.

In August Arthur visited the Ashdown Forest Hotel, not far from Monkstown, and the Leckie's family home. On the 10th Innes dined with Arthur and the Leckies, it can be assumed Jean was present. Then in September Arthur visited Kingsley as his school. Innes and Arthur dined with actor Lewis Waller. So while some account suggest a long dark sadness, Arthur, it seemed, resumed his social activities after Touie's death. One may see this as a way to deal with grief, and his activities so soon after her passing might not have turned a head.

But one thing would have nagged him; for years he had burned for Jean Leckie and now — what stood in their way from marriage? Propriety, at least, demanded he wait.

Arthur, The Detective

In November 1906 something captured Arthur's deepest attention. He grabbed his own deerstalker and pipe, ready to play detective. Arthur had received a letter from a young solicitor named George Edalji who begged Arthur to have his named cleared of a crime he claimed he did not commit.

George Edalji, the son of a Vicar, was accused of the mutilation of horses and cattle in Great Wryly. Additionally, he was said to have sent threatening letters, many of which were sent to his own home!

In reality it would not take Sherlock Holmes to solve this paper-thin case of racial prejudice, but local authorities were not playing fair and Arthur could see it. Mr Edalji was released on licence, which came as no surprise given the attention his case was getting. Though released he was still considered a criminal, and he wanted the author of Sherlock Holmes to help clear his name.

The Edalji family were already a subject of controversy. George's father had received many a hate letter in the past. The community included many small-minded people who resented a man of colour as Vicar. When George was 12, in 1888, his father received poison pen letters; after a while they stopped. In 1892 the letters resumed. They were penned by three different hands, all expressing their hatred for the Edaljis..

Chief Constable George Anson became aware of the situation with the Edalji family. Fueled by racial prejudice of his own, Anson did nothing to assist the family. A number of hoaxes and false claims were laid upon the Edalji family, some of which made George out to be a culprit. After years of threats and torment life was about to get even worse for the Edalji family.

1904 saw a strange outbreak of horse and cattle mutilations in the area. A total of 16 animals were discovered slashed by a sharp instrument across their stomachs. On the 18th of August a pony was discovered, in a muddy meadow, torn up, not far from the Vicarage. The police came to the house and demanded to see George's clothes. They took away razors, a damp coat, and a muddied pair of boots. The authorities claimed to have found horse hair on his clothing, and despite his father's account of George's whereabouts, which placed George in bed at the time of the mutilation, the police cared not, and George was arrested.

During the court case a handwriting expert named Thomas Henry Gurrin went on the record saying that George was responsible for the letters. When the prosecution searched for a motive, they found none. They then claimed that the crimes were done purely for recognition and driven by self-importance. George was sentenced to seven years in prison.

The case grew in the public eye and many attested to the lack of solid evidence. After three years in prison, George was released without explanation or pardon. He was still considered a convict, and under police watch. Not able to work or receive any aid, it was at this point George reached out to Arthur to help. With a number of people supporting him he needed someone on the case who could help clear his name in an attempt to get his life back.

Arthur met with George and discussed the case. As Arthur went through the trial notes he learned that the graphologist, George Gurrin, had already been responsible for sending an innocent man to prison. Arthur began a full on investigation which saw him retrace the steps of the pony slaughtering, interviewing George's father, and Captain Anson.

After Arthur gathered all the evidence he needed he came to a simple conclusion: the crimes committed were clearly not done by George and the local authorities' racial prejudice had ruined the life of an honest man. Arthur prepared a series of articles in the Daily Telegraph about the case debunking the evidence against Edalji. The First article was published on January 11, 1907.

The case gained momentum again. The media ran with the story and the public cries for justice forced the hand of the government to do something. As the case was appealed Arthur began receiving threatening notes by the same hand which the Edalji's had received. Arthur was not about the let the matter drop; he would find the real culprit.

Arthur discovered that a retired teacher had received a similar batch of hate letters. Arthur was able to make a connection between one of the pupils of the retired teacher and George's case. He suspected a man by the name of Royden Sharp, a known troublemaker, who had been expelled for letter forgery, worked as a butcher, and served on a cattle ship. Despite these suspicions, the case was cold, and the evidence he gathered on Mr Sharp did not hold up.

Nevertheless, in May 1907 George was granted a full pardon, even though some still believed George wrote the letters. Both Arthur and George's family were disgusted with the government for pardoning but not fully exonerating George.

While it was not the full outcome Arthur wanted, George was pardoned and free to resume his work. He moved to London where he worked as a solicitor for many years.

It is interesting to note that for more than twenty years, letters and cattle mutilations continued. Finally, in 1934 a labourer named Enoch Knowles was arrested and admitted to writing the letters and was sent to prison - but no one was ever arrested for the mutilations.

---

[12] *https://www.arthur-conan-doyle.com/index.php?title=File:The-New-York-Times-1905-11-19-conan-doyle-hard-luck-as-a-plawright.jpg*

Goodbye Undershaw, Hello New Horizon

Throughout Arthur's entire investigation Jean and her brother Malcolm were regular visitors to Undershaw. Jean had become a part of the family, and this pleased Arthur. Even his sister Connie and her husband had finally accepted Jean, and even invited Jean to their mother's 70th birthday in July 1907.

But it would have been unseemly for Arthur to remarry within less than a year of his wife's death. Jean was eager though, and would not wait much longer than 12 months.

One huge problem remained - Undershaw itself. How could Arthur and Jean forge a new life together in a house that was built for, and encapsulated the essence of his first wife, Touie?

The simple solution: Arthur bought a small villa near Ashdown Forest not far from Jean's parents. This would mark their new beginning, leaving the past behind.

In September 1907 Arthur, now 47, and Jean, 35, were quietly married at St Margaret's Church in Westminster. Innes was Arthur's best man, and his brother-in-law, Reverend Cyril Angell conducted the ceremony. Those in attendance were close relatives and friends. The wedding was a small, quiet affair, yet it was reported around the world.

The Daily Express stated that on the 9th Oct 1907, "Sir Arthur Conan Doyle had disposed of his house at Haslemere, and on return from their honeymoon he and Lady Doyle will take up their residence at Windlesham, Crowborough. Arthur leased Undershaw to a Mr Canon Edward Carus Selwyn, a retired headmaster."

"A few words may suffice to tell the little that remains."
- Doctor John H. Watson in The Final Problem [13]

Arthur retained ownership of Undershaw until 1921, though he and Jean never lived there. By this time, some 14 years into his marriage with Jean, Arthur had moved on. He'd continued writing and had built a new life with Jean. Undershaw perhaps served as a marker, a physical entity that tied him to a past which he and Jean struggled to release. He was ready to say goodbye to Undershaw and embrace his new life.

On the 10th May 1921 *The Times* stated that the house would go for a very low price to urge an immediate sale. Undershaw was sold for £4000, less than half than Arthur estimated he would get when he originally built the mansion. Arthur's new life would focus on the future and not the past; Jean was Arthur's life now. He had nine years ahead of him, happy years with Jean

and the birth of two more children. Undershaw had been a large part of his life during some of his most productive years and we can imagine him taking his leave of the grand old place.

Imagine, perhaps that tall, robust Scotsman walking slowly through the empty house. Stepping into his old study, one last time, where he wrote, in part and whole, so many great tales. Where the Hound of hell haunted the Baskervilles, where Sherlock Holmes emerged from those Swiss falls, where Sir Nigel, Brigadier Gerard and more came to life on the page. Perhaps he walked slowly down the hall into the dining-room and looked out the windows out onto the old tennis court, brushing his thick fingers along the windowpane.

In here, his entire family had once gathered to take a portrait, but how the children had grown since then.

The tinkle of soft piano music might have echoed in the now empty drawing-room.. But for a moment he might have glimpsed the upright piano and, Touie, happily tapping the keys with their children, Mary and Kingsley, still in his mind quite young, playing on the floor behind her. She, too, gazes out the open window before turning to look at Arthur with her ever-faithful smile. He smiles back at her just before the scene fades.

Arthur might then have moved slowly through the entrance hall, seeing the beautiful stained glass windows. Looking up the stairs he would remark upon the window where he quickly put a pictorial reference to the Foleys. He chuckled, perhaps, remembering how he tried to fix the error only to make another.

Might he then have kicked a stone as he walked up the drive, one last time, recalling how he cheated death when he toppled his car pulling in too fast.   Perhaps we would hear with him the echoes of gunfire and as he remembered his rifle club.

Undershaw, Arthur's home for Touie, that dear woman felled by tragedy who brought so much good into his life. For all of Arthur's struggles, and need for adventure, he cared deeply for her kind spirit and wanted the very best for her at all times.

This complex man - husband, father, and writer, might finally have stood at the top of the

---

13Taken from The Final Problem by Arthur Conan Doyle, Originally published by The Strand Magazine in1893.

drive looking down at an empty house and a quiet garden.. Sidney Paget, Bram Stoker, J.M. Barrie, William Gillette, all passed through that front entrance. The house held the memories of laughter and joy, heartache and sorrow. It was a house once alive with the Conan Doyle's rich lives, but now it would sleep.

Then with a wiggle of his moustache and clearing of his throat Arthur might have mustered up his final goodbye to that beautiful red brick mansion with a single comment. "Not bad, that?"

View from "Undershaw", Hindhead.

Chapter 7

Beyond Undershaw & The Legacy of Conan Doyle

Sir Arthur Conan Doyle was a remarkable man. From his early adventures as a seafaring Doctor to his exciting times with Dr Budd, setting up his own practice and becoming one of literatures greatest writers of not just detective stories but Napoleonic adventures and tales of knights and chivalry! He created unforgettable characters like Sherlock Holmes, Brigadier Gerard, and would go on to create the eccentric Professor Challenger.

His character of Sherlock Holmes would spawn thousands of continued adventures by crime writers all over the world through novels, comic books, films, and televison series. Sherlock Holmes would be at the birth of cinema starring in a silent film in 1916 and still be on our screens in 2016 with Benedict Cumberbatch, Robert Downy Jr, and Johnny Lee Miller simultaneously portraying the famous detective.

Arthur's influence has reached far and wide. He desperately wanted to be known for his serious and historic work, but he never really understood how serious and meaningful, and impacting, his Sherlock Holmes work was and would be. Yes, he knew he was a famous writer, he made his living from his stories. While I'm sure he would be hot under the collar to know now that he is most famous for that silly detective, Sherlock Holmes and his sidekick Doctor Watson, perhaps, in hindsight, if he could see the deep inspiration these and other characters he invited have he wouldn't be so hard on them.

Epilogue

Undershaw

It would not be long after Arthur left Undershaw that it went on to become a Hotel which lasted until 2004. The house went through minor changes, one being an extension to the eastern wing. It needed to adapt to the times. Undershaw remained a place of inspiration. Author Julian Barnes stayed at Undershaw to gather inspiration for his best selling novel Arthur & George, which later went on to become an ITV mini-series.

When the hotel closed, Undershaw sadly fell into rapid disrepair. Beaten down by the elements, extreme lack of care and upkeep, and diminished further by vandals, the house began to rot and become a ghostly shell of its former self. Windows were broken, the property was vandalised several times, and this once magnificent mansion began to crumble.

A group of avid Sherlockians and Conan Doyle experts known as the Undershaw Preservation Trust, led a movement to see the house restored to its former glory. At that time, the owners did not plan to restore the house and instead made plans for radical redevelopment. This once glorious home, filled with a rich history and memories, was on the verge of being split into town houses. Should this have happened the original Undershaw would have vanished completely.

A long game of tug-o-war ensued between the owners of Undershaw and the Undershaw Preservation Trust (UPT). UPT gathered momentum and support from fans of Sherlock Holmes and Arthur Conan Doyle all over the world. UPT's efforts to save the house were supported by Mark Gatiss, co-creator/writer/actor on BBC's hit series SHERLOCK, Stephen Fry and more. Many were passionate to see Undershaw restored.

From 2004-2012 the fight raged. In May 2012 the High Courts ruled against Undershaw's owners for not following proper planning permission protocols and their development plans were quashed. This left Undershaw in a state of limbo. What would happen next? Would the owners risk applying for planning permission and go through this again?

A flood of ideas were discussed as to what could happen to the house. Should it be a single dwelling and rarely opened to the public? Should it become a museum to Arthur Conan Doyle or an events and retreat for aspiring writers? You name it, the idea was brought up, but nothing could happen without proper financial support. How would Undershaw be saved?

David Forbes-Nixon (DFN) and Stepping Stones became the way forward. Stepping Stones, a local Hindhead school, with charitable status, and just a few minutes walk from Undershaw, was in desperate need of a bigger location to support the children. Stepping Stones was birthed when Larry Sullivan and Sandy Seagrove brainstormed the idea of a school that would better cater to children who needed more personal assistance in a learning environment.

Stepping Stones provides a first class education for children with hemiplegia, autism, chronic medical conditions and physical disabilities, and for children with mental and emotional issues.

With maximum capacity reached at their current location, in a converted church, Undershaw would give the school capacity to grow.

Undershaw was purchased for the school to be used as its main site. DFN did not jump into the purchasing of Undershaw lightly. Knowing full well that the house was built for Touie, a sufferer of tuberculosis, it catered perfectly to the school's needs for larger accommodation. DFN also understood the historical significance of the house and its original owner and he wanted to take extra care to ensure, as much as possible, the restoration and new additions would reflect the spirit and the history of the place.

Not only is Undershaw a place for children to learn, it is also a thriving, living memory and a symbol honouring Sir Arthur Conan Doyle, his wife Touie and their life and family. It is a monument to the Conan Doyle legacy.

Undershaw is alive again! It stands mighty and proud. Arthur used Undershaw as a place to do some of his greatest work, a haven for his family and their own special needs, as well as a centre for artistic gatherings, and for locals to come and learn life-skills. There is no doubt he would be pleased to see what has become of the beautiful house he left behind. A house that isn't remembered just for Sherlock Holmes, but for the man and his family who lived there. Undershaw lives on.

Miscellaneous Photographs of Arthur Conan Doyle, His Family and Sherlock Holmes

It was soon clear that there was no room inside a house for two heavy-weights, so we adjourned to the front lawn.

DR. CONAN DOYLE'S HOUSE.
From a Photo. by Elliott & Fry.

a period of
without the
identity leak
of these, wh
ment purcha
are in the
A bust of th
entrance hall
sons were all

VANITY FAIR Supplement

"Sherlock Holmes."

(Mr. William Gillette).

Mr HARRY YORKE BY ARRANGEMENT WITH Mr CHARLES FROHMAN —PRESENTS

SHERLOCK HOLMES

BY A. CONAN DOYLE AND WILLIAM GILLETTE.

THE GREATEST DRAMATIC SUCCESS OF THE TIMES.

Undershaw - A Journey Through Pictures
2012-2016

" Luke's First Visit to Undershaw in late 2012 "

" Construction Begins for Stepping Stones "

The dinning and drawing rooms with their marvellous South facing views

"Arthur's study where he wrote many classic stories"

"The beautiful stain glass window depicting the family crests"

"The second set of family crests Arthur hurriedly included and put the incorrect family motto"

"The spectacular view looking out towards the Surrey Hills."

Undershaw Now

Welcome to Undershaw

Bibliography / Sources

Memories and Adventures and Western Wanderings, Arthur Conan Doyle, Cambridge Scholars Publishing, Newcastle Upon Tyne, 2009.

A Life in Letters: Arthur Conan Doyle, Editors: Jon Lellenberg, Daniel Stashower & Charles Foley, Harper Perennial, London, 2008.

The Life of Sir Arthur Conan Doyle 2nd Edition, John Dickson Carr, Carroll & Graf Publishers, New York, 2003.

Conan Doyle: The Man Who Created Sherlock Holmes, Andrew Lycett, Phoenix, London, 2008.

The Adventures of Arthur Conan Doyle, Russell Miller, Harvill Secker, London, 2008.

An Entirely New Country: Arthur Conan Doyle, Undershaw, and the Resurrection of Sherlock Holmes, Alistair Duncan, MX Publishing, London, 2011.

www.bramstoker.org

www.arthur-conan-doyle.com

Photographs Courtesy

Wellcome library, London

British Library, London

Francis Frith Collection

Peter Harrington, London

Conan Doyle Collection, Portsmouth

Toronto Public Library

Roger Johnson

Luke Kuhns

Also from MX Publishing

MX Publishing is the world's largest specialist Sherlock Holmes publisher, with over two hundred titles and fifty authors creating the latest in Sherlock Holmes fiction and non-fiction.

The MX Book of New Sherlock Holmes Stories is the world's largest collection of new, traditional, Holmes stories, with all the authors donating their royalties to restoration projects at Stepping Stones.

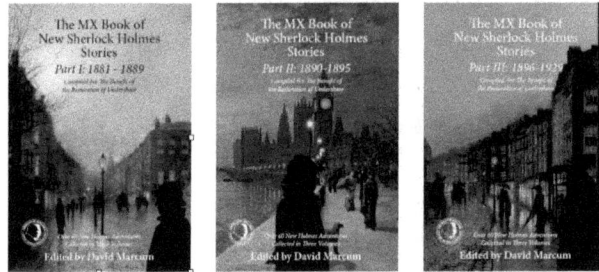

"This is the finest volume of Sherlockian fiction I have ever read, and I have read, literally, thousands."
Philip K Jones

Each volume has twenty or more stories and available in paperback, hardback and ebook formats. Volume five is launched for Chirstmas 2016 with more volumes coming in 2017.

www.mxpublishing.com

Also by Luke Kuhns

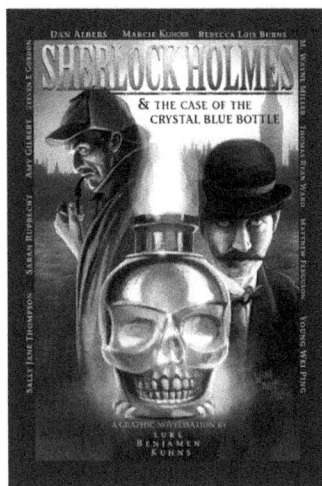

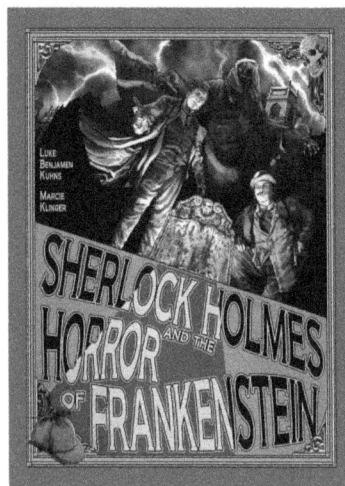

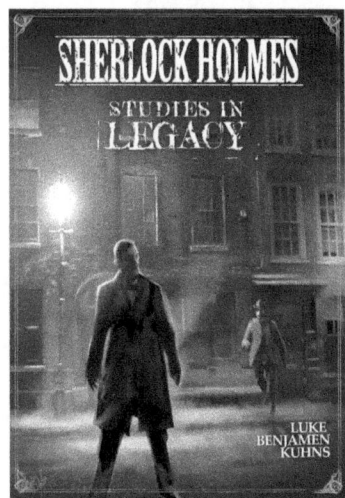

www.ingramcontent.com/pod-product-compliance
Lightning Source LLC
Chambersburg PA
CBHW050640150426
42813CB00054B/1124